W9-BXN-052

MY LOST MEXICO

BOOKS BY
JAMES A. MICHENER

Tales of the South Pacific
The Fires of Spring
Return to Paradise
The Voice of Asia
The Bridges at Toko-Ri
Sayonara
The Floating World
The Bridge at Andau
Hawaii
Report of the County Chairman
Caravans
The Source
Iberia
Presidential Lottery
The Quality of Life
Kent State: What Happened and Why
The Drifters
A Michener Miscellany: 1950-1970
Centennial
Sports in America
Chesapeake
The Covenant
Space
Poland
Texas
Legacy
Alaska
Journey
Caribbean
The Eagle and the Raven
Pilgrimage
The Novel
The World Is My Home: A Memoir
James A. Michener's Writer's Handbook
Mexico
My Lost Mexico

with A. Grove Day
Rascals in Paradise

with John Kings
Six Days in Havana

MY LOST MEXICO

by

JAMES A. MICHENER

with photographs by the author

STATE
HOUSE PRESS
1992

Library of Congress Cataloging-in-Publication Data

Michener, James A. (James Albert), 1907-
My lost Mexico / by James A. Michener ; with photographs
by the author.
p. cm.
ISBN 0-938349-93-7 (acid free paper).
ISBN 0-938349-94-5 (limit ed.) (acid free paper)
1. Michener, James A. (James Albert), 1907- Mexico. 2.
Michener, James A. (James Albert), 1907 - —Authorship.
3. Bullfights in literature. 4. Mexico in literature. 5.
Fiction—Authorship.

PS3525.I19M48 1992c
813'.54—dc 20   92-26953

Printed in the United States of America

First Edition

STATE HOUSE PRESS
P.O. Box 15247
Austin, Texas 78761

CONTENTS

A noiseless patient spider,
I mark'd where on a little promontory it stood isolated,
Mark'd how to explore the vacant vast surrounding,
It launch'd forth filament, filament, filament, out of itself,
Ever unreeling them, ever tirelessly speeding them.

—Walt Whitman

MY LOST MEXICO

I. SELECTING A SUBJECT

hen it became obvious in 1959 that my experimental novel *Hawaii*—experimental because it was so long and dealt with so many generations—was going to be well received, I naturally cast about to decide what subject I should tackle next. Two likely candidates surfaced as subjects for another long book.

The first possibility was Scotland, where in 1931-33 I had spent exciting years at the notable University of St. Andrews, very old, very rigorous and very Presbyterian. While there I had twice walked across the entire east-west breadth of the country, once from St. Andrews on the North Sea across to Oban on The Minch, an arm of the Atlantic Ocean, and once from Inverness down that glorious line of lochs, again to Oban. I had also spent much time in the Highlands, including a dramatic winter and a placid summer in the famous Outer Isles, the Hebrides in the far Atlantic, and particularly Barra, most colorful of the lot.

On site I had studied much Scottish history, especially the deplorable 'clearances' of the nineteenth century in which loyal and able Scottish crofters (peasants) were thrown off their traditional holdings by rich landowners, often with the excuse that the land was needed for hunting parties of vacationing gentlemen up from London. Many of the dispossessed emigrated to Nova Scotia, other parts of Canada and the United States, to the enormous enrichment of those new lands. While touring the Hebrides I memorized one of the anguished memorials of that cruel and vicious period:

> From the lone shieling of the misty island
> Mountains divide us and a world of seas.
> But still our hearts are true, our hearts are Highland
> And we in dreams behold the Hebrides.

I had done much work on the repulsive depopulation of the glens I had grown to love as I hiked along them, and in my reading I came upon a riveting story about another American in Scotland, a story that I longed to use some day if ever I taught or wrote about the clearances.

When Harriet Beecher Stowe shocked the conscience of America in 1852 with her anti-slavery novel *Uncle Tom's Cabin*, she became one of the contributory forces that made the Civil War inevitable. Her book was wildly successful both in America and Europe, was translated into twenty-three other languages, and made her an international heroine of liberal-thinking people. It was incomprehensible that only a few years later in 1856, when she traveled to England and Scotland to wild acclaim, her critical faculties seem to have become addled. Accepting social courtesies from the Duke of Sutherland and reveling in them, she blinded herself to his hideous behavior. As owner of vast estates in the northeast corner of Scotland, he was an arrogant leader among the group of wealthy land owners who evicted crofters whose families had rented the lands for generations. Bundling them up, often with police or military assistance, he drove them off his lands, refusing to worry about how or where they were to find another place to live.

He made himself anathema to decent Scots who felt that, whereas an owner did have certain rights to his lands, including hunting and the raising of cattle and sheep, he also inherited moral obligations to exercise those rights without harming poorer citizens who had served his forebears for generations. An understandable outcry rose against the Duke's unfeeling inhumanity, and he suffered a besmudged image and reputation which was more or less whitewashed by a stout defense of his policies written by his personal friend, the American abolitionist Harriet Beecher Stowe. Emotionally incapable of seeing that the clearances committed by a Scottish nobleman were just as intolerable as the slavery administered by a Georgia planter, she excused Sutherland's excesses as the mere and inescapable consequence of good land management. She deafened her ears to the wailing of the crofters as they went into exile; she rebuffed local protesters, applauded the police and ignored the arguments in defense of the dispossessed.

It was a remarkable instance in which a sensitive writer could see clearly the consequences of inhuman behavior at home, but failed to understand equal inhumanity when encountered abroad. Having known, in my Scottish travels, highlanders whose ancestors had been dispossessed during the clearances, and having heard and read about that tragic period, I was eager to use the Stowe affair as one vignette in the vast panorama of Scottish history, not the focal part by any means, but an illustrative one.

I have never been able to explain why I failed to write my Scottish novel. I knew the land, I knew the people, I knew the history, but the magic moment never came. I suspect it might have been because these experiences came too early in my life, my twenties, and before I had gained confidence in my ability to write. At any rate, in 1959 this powerful theme was again considered and rejected, never to be revived.

My second candidate for a subject was Mexico. As a student in Scotland in the early 1930s I had toured the Mediterranean as a deck hand aboard a Scottish coal freighter, and during my ship's layover in the little Spanish port of Burriana, where we picked up oranges to be taken back to Dundee for marmalade, I traveled south a few miles to Valencia, where I saw my first bullfight. Three notable matadors participated and gave such masterful performances that I became captivated by this art, brutal though it could be, and later traveled about Spain as a devotee of Domingo Ortega, one of the greatest matadors and a man whom I tried to imitate in my life and work habits: solid, wonderfully proficient, courageous, always his own man doing things his way, and sticking to the task long after his contemporaries had quit. I learned a lot from him.

It must have been in 1932 that I formulated a short story based on a gypsy bullfighter from Seville whose character was diametrically opposed to Ortega's. My man was a coward, a fraud, a simulator rather than an honest fighter, and a survivor because of his mastery of the professional tricks. Seeking a name for him, I came up with Gómez, which sounded amusing because of its long guttural first syllable and somewhat risible second. My man was Gómez and no other.

As I developed the story, not writing a line, the spirit of the tale centered on a paragraph of only four words. In presenting the matadors who were to play the significant roles, I visualized two of the most attractive and honorable heroes in the profession, one of them like Ortega, and after having presented them in favorable light I followed with this paragraph:

And there was Gómez.

In the following paragraph I planned to describe in sickening detail what a louse this long-legged, shifty, cowardly renegade was, and my imaginary story was underway.

I cherished that four-word paragraph because of the name's connotations, its hint of the ridiculous and the conniving cowardice with a proper touch of levity. Through the years, whenever I reconsidered that unborn short story, I could see Gómez and his failings and he became increasingly the hero of my tale. He never came to life; in 1932, since I was not yet a writer, I lacked the five thousand effective words to bring him into existence. But in 1936, while teaching in Colorado, I made my first excursion into Mexico, where I was captivated by the colorful life, the Spanish heritage, and the customs so different from what I had known in Pennsylvania. The memories of my brief trip to Spain and of my vivid experiences with bullfighting revived so vividly that in 1937 I returned to Mexico for the summer, returning again in 1938. During these protracted excursions I made friends with two unforgettable Mexican bullfighters, the taciturn Rolleri, one of the most accomplished assistants to a full-fledged matador, and a tall, slender *torero*, Flaco "Skinny" Valencia. With them I traveled the bullfight circuit—the rude *pachangas* in the country (pick-up affairs with no rules), the exhibitions, the *tientas* (testing of the cows for bravery), and the formal fights. They introduced me to a world that few strangers would be allowed to know.

In those years as I traveled widely throughout Mexico, I developed an amorphous plan to write about the peasant hero, Emiliano Zapata (1879-1919). In time I would live briefly in all the states of Mexico except only Quintana Roo in the extreme eastern edge of the Yucatán Peninsula (and even in Quintana Roo I would extensively explore the Mayan ruins in 1989). Thus I had acquired an intimate knowledge of many aspects of Mexican life, reinforced by wide reading in Mexican studies. In 1937, imbued with the color and drama of Mexico and its bullrings, I drafted a compact novel on bullfighting as I had observed it in Mexico. I featured the matador Gómez, and with considerable hope I submitted it to Harold Latham, the charismatic editor-in-chief of The Macmillan Publishing Company, the man who had discovered *Gone With the Wind* while on an exploratory trip looking for publishable manuscripts. When he reached Denver on a subsequent trip, I offered him my truncated novel, but he graciously declined: 'Not quite ready, but it shows promise. Come back later.'

Since these experiences were even more recent than the Scottish—the late 1930s and early 40s as opposed to 1933—and equally intense, it was understandable that in 1959 when searching for a new subject I would think of Mexico. As soon as possible I finished my corrections on the galleys of *Hawaii*, put them behind me and cleansed my mind of South Pacific matters. With a fiery desire to get back to Mexico, to my bullfighting friends and to the research materials, in the late months of 1959 my wife and I drove down to Mexico City in the lovely days when one could still breathe the air. We had the good fortune to find a room in the ancient Hotel Cortés on the north side of the wooded *Alameda,* the large park in the center of town. There, in the enclosed patio of the hotel, an early nineteenth century Spanish haven with a singing fountain, I plunged into the massive task I had set myself.

It was a rewarding time as I reintroduced myself to Mexican custom and history. The old hotel was an admirable place to do such work, for it bespoke the periods I would want to write about. I also met new Mexican friends to enrich my knowledge. Although with passing years Rolleri and Flaco Valencia were no longer available, I became acquainted with a new generation of matadors, especially the artist with the cape, Alfonso Ramírez, who fought under the name Calesero, and Pepe Luis Vásquez, one of the bravest of modern matadors.

Calesero invited me to a grand three-day festival which he was masterminding in his home city of Aguascalientes, and there in the spring of 1960 I caught the first glimmer of what my proposed Mexican novel would have to be: a three-day taurine festival in some smaller Mexican city. But Calesero's Aguascalientes did not attract me, for when I studied its history I found that although it was attractively old, its major claim to notoriety was General Santa Anna's perpetuation of a gruesome slaughter near there in 1835. I did not like Santa Anna nor his wanton killing, so Aguascalientes could not be my locale.

But as I was driving back to Mexico City I recalled something a Mexican scholar had told me: 'If you want to catch an unsullied glimpse of what Mexico was like in colonial days, the place to go is the old mining city of Guanajuato.' Now, catching a brief look at my road map, I saw to my surprise that the town lay only a short distance off the highway I was traveling, and a quick detour led me to a gem, the site for which I had been searching.

Guanajuato was a colonial city graced by old buildings of excellent architecture, the remnants of an aqueduct, and at the

Aqueduct

edge of town a deep hole in the earth, an unprotected, un-rimmed, abandoned mining shaft over whose edge I lay, awestruck by the drop below me. As I stared down into the darkness I found another portion of the structure of my proposed novel. Transfixed by the limestone walls of the shaft and their ancient scars, I listened as the old man who was showing me the place said: 'In the old days when we sent so much silver to the king of Spain, the ore had to be carried by workers like slaves, up these winding stairs that reached deep into the earth. Women were the beasts of burden, climbing the stairs barefoot with baskets of ore perched on their heads. Sometimes they fell, for the stairs were not good.' He added: 'The work below was done by men who used donkeys to move the ore. Once a donkey was lowered down on ropes, he never again saw daylight or cropped grass in a meadow.'

In that moment, as we lay picturing the immense depth up which chains of little Indian women had lugged their heavy burdens, the central segment of my novel sprang to life. In my studies I had read about the large numbers of southern gentlemen who had fought on the side of the South during the Civil War and who had refused to remain in the United States under the possibility that the hated Ulysses S. Grant might become president. Some had fled to Canada, becoming good citizens there, but more had come south to Mexico where, too, they fitted in. The principal character of my novel, the narrator but not the hero, would be the grandson of such a Confederate loyalist who had finished his life in the Guanajuato region as supervisor of a silver mine. There had been such men, and I could build my novel around one of them, but even as I made the decision I realized that I was still working backward.

I now had the ending of my novel, the three-day taurine fair in a small city like Guanajuato, and the middle portion, the operation of the silver mine in the nineteenth century, but I did not have a reasonable beginning. And because I had spent so much time on geology in *Hawaii,* I rejected the idea of reaching so far back as to describe the genesis of the great volcanoes that marked the region east and south of Guanajuato. What incidents in the ancient history of Mexico would I use to start the novel? I had inadequate knowledge to make a sensible choice.

Aware of my ignorance, I put all else aside and gave myself an intensive seminar in Mexican pre-Columbian history, a study which took me first to the great Aztec pyramid of Teotihuacán where I spent most of a week trying to visualize what life must have been like in those days. In Mexico City I haunted the notable museum of ancient Mexican art, architecture and pre-history. While working there I was told of a Toltec site more instructive than the great pyramid, and when I visited Tula, some fifty miles north of Mexico City, I saw one of the gems of the Western Hemisphere, the relic of a civilization that produced wonders, the outline of a city that must have contained thousands of citizens whose houses, shops and gardens have vanished. What remains are stone remnants of buildings, rows of gigantic male figures fifteen feet high and carved out of a very pale pink stone. But what captivated me most was a low

The mine and its pyramid

Entrance to the silver mine

Pyramid of sacrifices

Jaguar

statue whose type was common throughout central Mexico, a
Chac Mool, an extraordinary human figure which once seen can
never be forgotten. A kind of bullyboy, handsomely carved and
proportioned, the statue's head is always twisted so that the chin
rests directly over either the left or right shoulder. He is lying
on his back except that his elbows support his upright torso,
while his knees are bent so that his stomach forms a level
platform parallel to the earth. On his stomach-platform rests a
beautiful stone bowl of some size. The bowl is there to receive
the hearts torn from the chests of living men. The *Chac Mool*
and what he represents is loathsome, but I was deeply affected
by him.

As a result of my work at Tula I met a delightful Frenchman
whose ancestors had come to Mexico from Barcelonette, a
village in the French mountains bordering on Italy. He was
even more interested in archaeology than I and arranged for me
to participate in one of the most rewarding expeditions I would
ever take. Under the tutelage of Mexico's premiere expert on

Jaguar

the Mayan period, we flew to a small airfield cut out of the jungles in eastern Mexico, from where in creaking old cars we journeyed into a dense tropical forest which hid the great ruins of Palenque. We were there just as the wonders of this remote spot were being uncovered: massive temples, huge walls covered with Mayan hieroglyphics, a soaring public building of some kind and, uncovered not long before my visit, a subterranean tomb covered by a stone slab of massive dimension and weight under which lay hidden artifacts and jade relics more than a thousand years old. It was a sobering thought that here in the jungles of Mexico had flourished a civilization with notable architecture, governmental procedures over states and principalities, written records, astronomical time keeping and individual works of art, when their Indian cousins in the future United States had not yet reached a level of civilization in which they could produce any of these things. Palenque, as I saw it when it was just being reclaimed from the jungle, exerted a profound influence on me. I would have to begin my novel with a glimpse of earliest pre-Columbian Indian life, although I would not use the Mayas.

As a result of these various studies conducted intensively and over a substantial period of time, I judged that I was almost ready to start serious work on the Mexican segments of my novel, but two serious gaps remained in my knowledge. Until they were filled I could not feel confident. One was the Civil War background of my American-Mexican narrator, the other the pre-Cortés background of his Spanish ancestors, so I traveled north to explore the battle sites of the Civil War.

I had originally planned to have my 1850 American family living on the Mississippi River in the town of Natchez, from where my protagonist of that period would travel north in the Confederate ranks to fight the battle of Vicksburg against General Grant, who would serve admirably as one of the villains of my novel. I spent much time along the river, making myself reasonably well informed on the town life of Natchez-under-the-Hill, the character of the Natchez Trace, the famous old trail through the wilderness, and the cruel siege of Vicksburg in which life was held in such low regard. When I felt that I was moderately well qualified to write about these matters, a curious thing happened, one with which other writers will be familiar.

I developed a strong feeling that the Mississippi River was not the setting in which my narrator's family would have been at ease. They had to be Georgians or Carolinians or, best of all from the point of view of my needs, Virginians, so I left the great river and drove eastward to the region around Richmond, Virginia. There the countryside northeast of the Confederate capital, the Wilderness of the Civil War, provided me with exactly what I sought: a battlefield of crucial importance and the scene of General Grant's callous misuse of his northern troops, sacrificing thousands needlessly, as well as a nearby southern city with a lively social life. By the time I left Richmond I believe I understood what had happened at Cold

Pre-Columbian stelae

Harbor, and I needed to look no further for an explanation of why my Confederate officer, despite his great victory there, would surrender his citizenship in a nation led by Grant.

Last in line of my researches was the Spanish component, and as I studied ways in which I might get to Spain for a review of sixteenth century facts I knew only vaguely, I found in a Sunday paper an offer I could not believe: 'Come to Spain. We fly you over in a new four-engined jet. When you land at Madrid we give you a car, free, for two weeks, and a tankful of gas. To top it off, we give you, also free, three nights board and room in hotels of first category. All for $315.' I grabbed at the offer, and the Spanish Travel Office not only fulfilled every promise but promoted me to first class on the flight over because of overcrowding on the inexpensive seats offered in the ad. What a way to travel to Spain!

In that congenial country I had two obligatory targets: Salamanca, the handsome university town in which my narrator's Spanish ancestors would have flourished; and Seville, from where in the early 1500s they would have left for Mexico. My days were joyous in the former city, renowned for its medieval quality and its superb central square, for I had often visited there in the past and could visualize my characters as they must have been in the early sixteenth century. By the time I left, I knew what had happened in Salamanca, one of my favorite cities in the world.

In Seville my requirements were less demanding since it played only a marginal role in the proposed novel, and the sights about which I wanted to refresh my memory were quickly covered. I was about to fly home when, one evening as I wandered near the massive cathedral with its Moorish bell tower, the *Giralda,* I saw coming toward me in the plaza a tall young fellow whose arrogant bearing was so unmistakably that of a bullfighter that I almost cried aloud: 'That's got to be him! He's from Philadelphia!'

Some years earlier I had seen, in a bullfight magazine

published in the United States, the handsome photograph of a young American from Philadelphia, John Fulton Short, who had undertaken the heartbreaking task of becoming a *matador de toros* in Spain. After an apprenticeship in Mexico where he became proficient, he tested his fortune in Spain. He had the physique and posture to be a matador, but whether he had the skill I could not, of course, have an opinion. Two newspaper stories assured me that he did.

For several years thereafter his photograph lingered in my mind, for since I knew of the incredible barriers that prevent even Spanish or Mexican *muchachos* from succeeding in the ring, I was aware that for an American to achieve success would be almost impossible, and I thought: 'Good luck, matador!'

Now, as I left the cathedral, a gigantic, brooding structure big enough to serve all of southern Spain, I saw the graceful young man of the photograph. Hastening to his side I asked: 'Aren't you John Fulton Short, the American bullfighter?' and proudly he stiffened and said he was.

I stress the word *proudly* because if a young man who aspires to be an arrogant, posturing bullfighter does not have an inherent pride in his bearing and confidence in his skill, he will have no chance whatever of becoming a matador. Arrogance is the plasma that keeps the blood of the matador functioning, and without it he becomes limp.

That chance encounter, which came about because I remember striking photographs and can recall them almost at will, launched a friendship which has lasted over thirty years. It carried consequences I could not have foreseen because Matador Fulton, as he was called professionally, occupied student digs with another young American, Robert Vavra of San Diego, who had an amazing skill in photographing animals, especially horses, and something others could not capture on film, the elusive unicorn. Since I had no idea what a competing photographer was talking about when he snorted contemptiously: 'Simple. All you need to snare a unicorn is composite developing techniques,' I preferred to believe that Robert had found a family of unicorns somewhere in the magical regions of southern France, because he did have photographs of them.

Some years later Vavra's poetic cameras would illustrate my book about Spain, and with that conspicuous start he would move ahead to become perhaps the world's outstanding photographer of animals, and one of the very good authors of nature books and children's stories.

How fortunate I was that evening to meet two such talented young men. In subsequent years I traveled with them to all corners of Spain as people joked: 'Short is tall. It's Vavra who's short.' In time John Fulton succeeded in becoming a full-fledged Spanish matador, while Vavra acquired one of the fine country ranches outside Seville. The three of us spent many hours at bull ranches. It is strange, and a fact of note, that a young bull can have as his unquestioned father some great bull full of years and parading his muscle, and handsome to a degree which makes the uninitiated watcher cry: 'There's a master bull! If he ever went into the plaza he'd tear it apart. His offspring must be terrors.'

Not so. The appearance of this formidable seed bull does determine how his male offspring will look, noble and manly, but the character of the young bull will stem mainly—and some claim totally—from his mother. If she is brave, he will be. If she proves cowardly so will he, so it is exciting to attend a *tienta* at a rural ranch which breeds fighting bulls, for some of the young cows to be tested will prove to be absolute tornadoes, not only willing but positively eager to attack anything that moves, while their blood sisters will be totally lacking in character.

Back at the bullrings of the towns, Fulton, Vavra and I would haunt the corrals studying the animals for the Sunday fight, then prowling the sorting area on Sunday morning trying to estimate which of the six bulls would do well that afternoon and which would prove either obstinate or cowardly. With

At the bull ranch

such tutelage I became a modest expert on taurine behavior.

My studies completed, I felt qualified to begin laying out the plan for a substantial novel. On one sunny Thursday afternoon, accompanied by my tutors, I crossed the bridge which leads from Seville to its gypsy quarter, *Triana*, on the far side of the Guadalquivir River. There in what I then called a wine shop, but which I would later know as a *tapa* bar where wine and trays filled with things like squid, octopus, boiled eggs, anchovies and a wilderness of salads were served on tiny saucers, I had a detailed vision of the novel I hoped to write. Leaving the *tapa* bar momentarily, I crossed the street to a stationery store where I bought a schoolboy's notebook, on the first page of which I began the outline of my Mexican novel.

It contained, at that time, twenty-two chapters, obviously too many, so that cutting and consolidation became imperative. The page following this shows the original workbook entry which launched the novel, and it demonstrates how painfully decisions are made. The parenthesized numbers from 1 through 12 were added by me in 1992 as I prepared these notes.

OPENING   1961

This section started in Seville,
Thursday, March 30, 1961
AT THE WINE SHOP IN
TRIANA

(1) Altomecs Toltecs 500 A.D.   GRAL. GRUE   1913

Aztecs Altomecs 1250   FATHER LOPEZ 1928

                              (8) SEVILLE   1933

(2) Salamanca's   1540   (9) THE FAT BOY   1938-1961

Cathedral   1640   THE FIRST AFTERNOON FIGHT 1961

(3) Aqueduct   1746   (10) THE BEATNIK 1951-1961

(4) Mines
Aqueduct →1740   (12)   THE SECOND AFTERNOON FIGHT 1961

No good or straight
chronology. No
full. Too close.
Hawaii
structure
STRUCTURE

FACADE   1760   THE BULL   1904-1961

GANADERIA   1830   THE POET   1925-1961

(5) GETTYSBURG 1863   THE THIRD AFTERNOON FIGHT 1961

(6)   HOUSE OF TILE
THE ~~BARRACKS~~ 1865   (11) MRS. GARY Ramsay   1961

(7) THE LEALS   1886

Following them will give you a guide to my thought processes. (1) The two Indian chapters would be radically changed. I wanted the novel to begin in A.D. 500 so I required a tribe much earlier than my imaginary Altomecs, who did not coalesce as an organized group until later. I substituted the Toltecs but never used them, for I needed someone even earlier. For the later tribe, on the eve of the Old World's discovery of the New, I decided to avoid the Aztecs, since their history was well known, and I replaced them with the Altomecs, a vigorous tribe to which I had developed a deep attachment. I knew the Altomecs, their history, their architecture, their tribal customs, and their deities, since I had invented them. (2) Since consolidation of chapters was inescapable, I cut the six chapters beginning with Salamanca and ending with Ganadería, substituting for them one concise chapter. (3) I have always believed the word *acqueduct* was properly spelled with two c's. (4) I had already decided my silver mine would be called *Mineral,* the *Mineral de Toledo.* (5) Despite all the work I had done at Natchez and Richmond, by the time I started my novel I had reconsidered and decided that the battle of Gettysburg would prove the most rewarding. What a foolish mistake that was, initiated perhaps by the Spanish wine. It lasted only a few weeks. (6) The House of Tile is shown here as built in 1865 but was actually constructed three centuries earlier. (7) I was, as always, insecure about names. Leal for my Spanish-style bullfighting family would survive to the end, as would López for my heroic priest. But the name for my revolutionary general would vary numerous times during the next thirty years. Originally he was Grug, then Frug, then Freg, and then other names. Neither the general nor Father López would retain their separate chapters. (8) My entry for a separate chapter on Seville is an enigma to me thirty years later. What I had planned for this city, other than as the Old World origin of the Spanish Palafox family, must remain a mystery. (9) The fat boy disappeared early. (10) Neither the beatnik, the bull nor the poet would be given separate chapters. (11) And I'm fumbling around for the right name of the Oklahoma woman I liked so much. Here she's lost Gary and is trying Ramsay. That won't last, either. (12) The entry which today seems most important in whipping the novel into shape is the one containing those ominous warnings: 'No good as straight chronology. Too close to *Hawaii* structure.' In obedience to this warning, I went back to the top of the page and wrote, in red ink, a superseding entry 'Opening 1961.' It would certainly include something about cactus and maguey, for they would form the ideological framework of the novel.

It was easy to proclaim 'I'll start in 1961 with something about the two symbolic plants of Mexico,' but it was much more demanding to answer the question: 'Yes, but how should the narrative itself begin?' for the task ahead would be long and complicated. Then, one sunny day as I motored about exploring the back roads of Guanajuato—my imaginary city of Toledo—I saw ahead of me two Indian women, wearing shawls and walking from their little village to the market in Guanajuato. They were so poetic in their movements, so inherently a part of their land that I cried aloud: 'That's it! Two women on their way to town carrying the things they have to sell.' And throughout the long life of this manuscript, covering thirty-one years of productive work, disarming failure and magical recovery, those two Indian women maintained their slow, lovely walk through my mind. They are the soul of my book.

One aspect of that first outline drafted in *Triana* startles me as I review it today. Nowhere are the three young women from Texas mentioned, yet they would be the focus of the final chapters and the cause for endless hours of revision. I'm sure I must have considered them in the general outlining of the narrative but had perhaps fitted them in elsewhere. At this juncture I believed there could be no proper conclusion to the novel without them.

But the overall thrust of the novel had been visualized and

roughly laid out. With the notebook in hand I returned to Mexico City, taking up quarters in the delightful María Cristina, a semi-modern hotel built in this century, where I started taking the photographs and assembling the notes I would require. The drafting of the novel was underway.

Cactus

II. HARD WORK

I had reached only a few pages in the writing when I realized that my original outline for the novel was faulty in many respects, and even when I opened with my main character on the highway to my Mexican town of Toledo, I became completely muddled as to how the main narrative should proceed. I therefore redrafted the entire outline as shown in the left-hand column of the next page. As I look today upon this bizarre arrangement of the first seven chapters (numbered 1-7 in the left-hand column) I cannot recall what tortured reasoning produced such a solution.

The reason for the confusion was a literary one: I had not yet built a satisfactory framework within which the narrative could unfold. The idea of dealing with the bullfighting Leal family as the first major presentation, followed by histories of the Spanish Palafox family and then my Indian matador, was stupid, to phrase it gently. Not only a poor sequence for providing the reader with basic understanding, it was also aesthetically unrewarding. Nor did I yet see that whatever I said about the Spanish Palafoxes would contain and preempt the strong material on Salamanca. Looking at this jumble today, I cannot be proud.

The remainder of the left-hand column is equally inept, except that I have now established Veneno as my barber who reprehensibly shaves the horns of the fighting bulls to protect his matador son. The relationships between the three fights, Friday, Saturday, Sunday, and the events that transpired in the hours between, are beginning to take shape. I had great plans for the Rooster, an amiable hanger-on at the bullring, but he developed no staying power. We have Cold Harbor in a logical place, but note that I still wanted to call it Gettysburg, and the

1. OPENING KILOMETER 7.

2. THE LEALS

3. PALAFOX

4. THE INDIAN

5. THE DRUNKEN BUILDERS (700-1200) ⎫
   THE ALTOMECS   (1200-1524)   ⎬ DONE
   8 SALAMANCA   (1524-1588)   ⎭ MUST COME BEFORE COLD HARBOR

6. THE CRITIC

7. THE FIRST BULLFIGHT

8. ECLIPSES OF   (Have him in Cordoba [parade])
   DEATH   Seville?
   Venero (Darbor)
   ~~city~~ COLD HARBOR (1864)

   THE AMERICANS

   THE SECOND BULLFIGHT

   BY TORCHLIGHT (bull, Leal / Don't)

   the Rooster (Seville?)

   the Bull
   Seville - Travel...
   the Third Fight...

   Mrs. Ramsay

9 Barber
10 Spanish Architecture
11 Cold Harbor
11 American
12 Saturday Fight
13 By Torchlight
15? The Sorting
16 the Bull
17 Seville
18 Sunday Fight
19 Mrs. Evans.

evening's torchlight theatrical is both properly named and placed. What Seville is doing in there I still cannot at this remove imagine—it must have been a pitifully wrong idea—but Mrs. Ramsay, still without her proper name, is prominent at the end of the book, as I always planned.

Taking the left-hand column in toto, it is a miserable plan. However, in the right-hand column of this same page I was making a substantial advance in whipping this culminating material into shape. Of the eleven titles shown, the first two, *Barbers* and *Spanish Ancestors*, pertain to the first half of the narrative, and were securely placed. The remaining nine, 11-19, would ultimately be compressed to seven; *The Bull* and the mysterious *Seville* would be dropped; 11 and 14 would become *American Ancestors*, first in Virginia and then in Mexico. Despite the nearly accurate arrangement, the three young women from Texas have not yet made their appearance, and this bewilders me, but Mrs. Evans has found her proper name.

The next work page, done some months after the preceding, demonstrates how, during the course of actual composition, ideas and possibilities change wildly. The corrections in the left-hand column deal with a mélange of ideas, especially the finding of the right names for my characters. Victoriano Leal, Palafox and Veneno would survive through all changes. Others were extremely fugitive. The innkeeping Viuda, a widow, would soon become part of the Palafox family. El Lobo, my Indian matador, became Juan Gómez on this page. Senaquerib, a *nom de plume* I fancied for my critic, would later become León Ledesma, much better for repeated appearance in narrative. Father Sánchez would revert to the original Father López. Manuel Gómez, the engineer, would vanish. My narrator's father, here George Forrest, would become John Clay, and his book would be retitled *The Pyramid and the Cathedral.* The revolutionary general would undergo six or seven changes; here it is Grug, then Frug, and neither was worth serious consideration.

VIUDA (~~Pettit~~) ~~Mier~~ Patti , the innkeeper   THE INNKEEPER   25

VICTORIANO LEAL, ~~the Sicilian~~   THE GYPSY

DON ~~Kinley~~ FAUSTO PALAFOX Y MIER, the ~~Spanish~~ Rancher   THE RANCHER
JUAN GOMEZ EL LOBO, the Indian   THE INDIAN

~~FATHER SANCHEZ, the Priest~~

THE FIRST FIGHT   THE FIRST DAY
SENAQERID, THE CRITIC   THE CRITIC
CORD CABOT, the BIBLICAL SCHOLAR   THE SCHOLAR

VENENO, THE PICADOR   THE PICADOR

, THE WOULD-BE FIGHTER   THE AMERICANS

THE SECOND FIGHT   THE SECOND DAY

BLACK MOUTH, the Bull   THE BULL

MICHAEL GREGORY, the Expense Account   THE EXPENSE ACCOUNT
FATHER SANCHEZ, THE PRIEST   THE PRIEST
MANUEL GOMEZ, the ENGINEER   THE ENGINEER
ROOSTER OF MEXICO   THE ROOSTER
THE THIRD FIGHT   THE THIRD DAY

THE HOUSE OF TILE   THE HOUSE OF TILE

GEORGE FORREST THE PYRAMID AND THE PRIEST

GENERAL ~~Gross~~ FRUG   17

Most significant among these names are 'Cord Cabot, the Biblical Scholar,' and 'Michael Gregory, the Expense Account.' The first, an American professor doing research in Mexico on the revolution in the early 1900s who had a learned knowledge of the role of the Catholic Church in that period, perished early; his major concerns would be voiced by the one-armed poet who wrote the drama that will appear in the printed version as *By Torchlight*.

Michael Gregory will also vanish as a name. Unfortunately, the more euphonious name Cord Cabot will survive as that of the Hollywood actor who fiddles with his expense account. It is this and subsequent attempts to include Hollywood personae that will ultimately account for the abandonment of this manuscript in late 1961. This page, 169, is thus both a testament to the hard work a writer does but also a monument to a disastrously wrong turn such effort can take. After thirty years it stares back at me as a reminder of the worst miscalculation I ever made as a writer.

In the right-hand column, done some days later, I see that I have the first six chapters, beginning with the innkeeping widow, not in perfect order but close to it. The gypsy is my elegant matador Victoriano Leal; the rancher is my breeder of fighting bulls; the Indian is my native Indian matador, less elegant but more instinctively brave than Victoriano. The critic, who is one of my favorite characters in the narrative, is moved forward so that his reflections will assist the reader in understanding details in the first fight, and this was a productive shift. However, *The Scholar* and *The Picador* will be dropped as chapters; *The Americans*—my Texas girls are now on the scene!—come far too early, and the fight on the second day has not been properly prepared for. More serious, the barbering incident has not yet been inserted into the plan. But these corrections would be easily made, so I was justified in being pleased with progress on these chapters of the book.

The last seven proposed chapters starting with *The Bull* are a disaster. The first five of these seven will be totally dropped from the final version, glaring proof of an inadequate preparation of the story line. And three subjects which will be most productive in the final version are not even mentioned: the torchlight drama in the plaza, the detailed chapters on the American ancestors, and the sorting of the bulls as preparation for the maiming of the heroic bull by the Leals.

The significant point is that I had all these matters in the recesses of my mind—they had been there for many years—but I had not yet found the proper way to present them. This page, then, is painful proof of the hard reasoning required by any serious piece of writing. Writing is usually a process of fits and starts, and when intrusive elements like Hollywood actors thrust their way in, it can take months or even years to correct the error. This time it required three decades.

The first steps toward salvation, however, were drafted some months following the above impasse in the planning. This time I had the ten opening chapters in almost perfect order, not surprising since I had already started composition. As I worked from chapter to chapter, I knew quite clearly where I was heading. But my thought processes were not clarified regarding the rest of the narrative. This attempt was so addled it contained several chapters I would ultimately have to discard; there was still a full chapter on the bull, which would have been tedious, and the strange diversion to Seville persisted. I had begun to think of my delightful oil widow from Tulsa as Mrs. Evans, but in a later list of chapters she reverted to Mrs. Ramsay. The left hand column of this page reveals I was far from solving the problem of how to proceed with the book. Nevertheless, in the column on the right I had already begun to estimate the number of pages which each chapter would require—at well over 800 pages, obviously too long!

Although I was bogged down in my planning of specific chapters, I retained a clear understanding of the data I would need to write the book, so during these days of indecision, most

	J.A.☆	Typist
1 Cactus + Maguey	32	(26)
2. The Spaniard	54	(48)
3. the Rancher	49	(38)
4. The Indian	71	(59)
5. the Indian Ancestors	85	(66)
6. the Critic	62	(54)
7. Friday Fight	56	(44)
8. The Meaning of Death	54	(43)
9. The Barbers	29	(25)
10. Spanish Ancestors	91	(78)

578 pages →

ESTIMATE

? ? ??		
the Americans 11	30	16
Saturday Fight 12	35	19
By Torchlight 13	35	19
Anglo-Saxon Ancestors 14	168	116
the Battery } 15	30 }	× 22
the Bull }	85 }	
SEVILLE :	50	×
Sunday Fight 16	30	16
Mr. Evans 17	30	16
	813	

$$\frac{5}{223} = \frac{15}{840} : \frac{72}{29,100} = \frac{890}{350,000}$$

HAWAII 45 l/p × N w.p = [530] n.pp

$$\frac{350,000}{520} = 660 \text{ pages for FIESTA}$$

James A. Michener in Seville. Illustration by Matador John Fulton.

of them spent at the María Cristina Hotel in Mexico City or on trips to Spain, I filled two notebooks with unorganized bits of information: rough outlines of chapters, chronologies, numerous sketches and maps, and whatever else might prove useful. The notebook I had started that day in *Triana's* wine shop had 130 jumbled pages; the second, purchased in Mexico, ran to an additional 114; a third contained only photographs I had taken in Spain and Mexico. They served as abbreviated notes.

A selection of those varied pages will summarize the work I was doing while my ideas were maturing. Basic to the story was the physical setting: the environs of my imaginary city of Toledo and its central plaza in which so much of the action occurs (pps. 32-33); careful depictions of the deep mine on which the prosperity of the city depended (pps. 34-35); and the three dominating structures, pyramid (p. 36), cathedral (p. 37) and aqueduct (p. 38). Each of these obligatory sketches required numerous redraftings as the story unfolded, but only in the case of the mine do I here provide two versions. For the mine there was a total of six versions before I got it right; as each new piece of evidence became available, the depths of the various levels had to be adjusted, as did the structures of the lateral caves .

The Environs Of Toledo

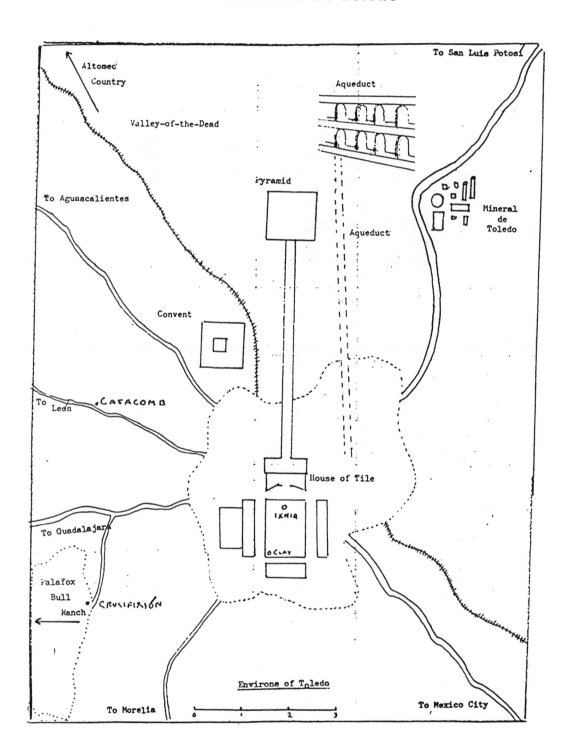

The Central Plaza

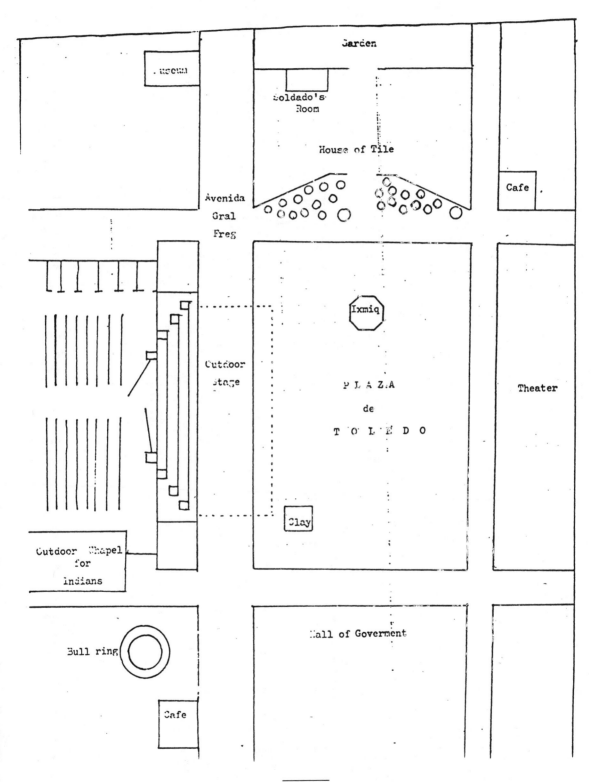

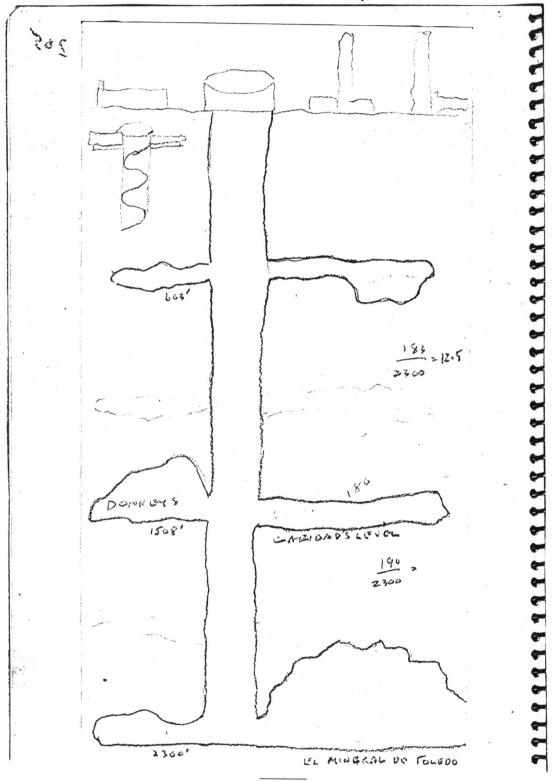

Mineral de Toledo—Final Configuration

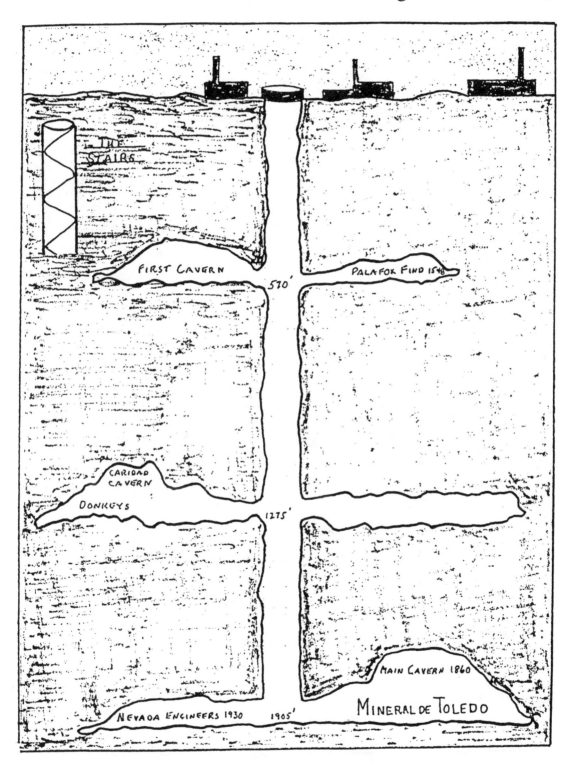

Pyramid : 219″ feet high

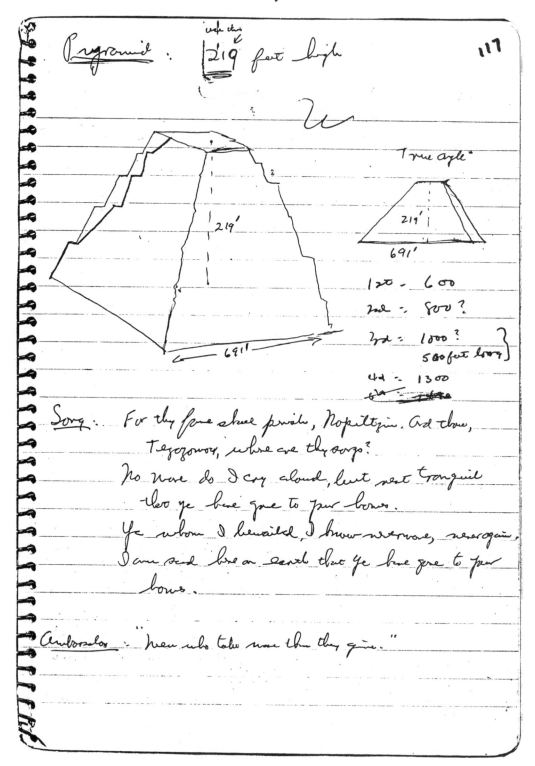

True angle

219′

691′

219′

691′

1st - 600
2nd - 800 ?
3rd - 1000 ?
   500 feet long
4th - 1300

Song : For they shall perish, Nopiltzin. And thou,
Tezozomoc, where are thy songs?
No more do I cry aloud, but rest tranquil
that ye have gone to your homes.
Ye whom I bewailed, I know nevermore, never again,
I am sad here on earth that ye have gone to your
homes.

Ambrosalos : "men who take more than they give."

The Cathedral

The Aqueduct

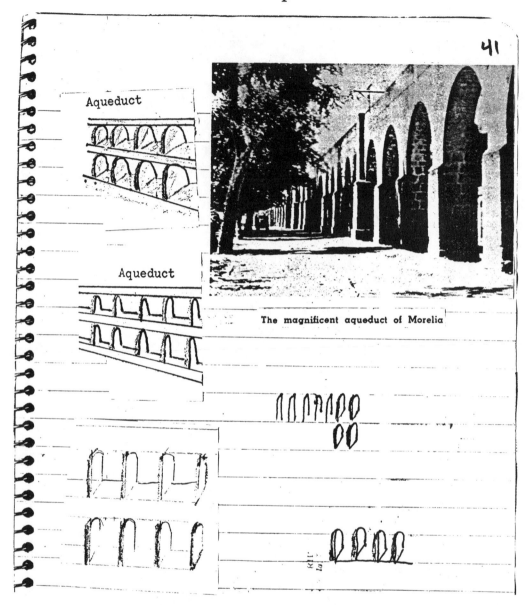

The magnificent aqueduct of Morelia

As I labored over my sketches of the physical setting I was spending equal time on the maturing of my characters. To keep this multitude of human beings from varied times and cultures in order, I devoted sixteen pages of my notebook to the years A.D. 500 to 1960, and two pages from that chronology are shown (pps. 40-41), also the two pages on which the histories of my two competing matadors are developed (pps. 42-43).

I soon became aware that I had to expand my knowledge of the art of bullfighting, so I returned to Spain, went down to Seville, and spent many hours with John Fulton, the American matador, and Robert Vavra, the photographer of unicorns. To get as close as possible to the life of the bulls and the history of their development, we went first to the historic ranch of Concha y Sierra, a name revered in taurine history, where the present owners gave us the run of their holdings. While there I devised the history of Marinero and Sangre Azul, two bulls I would be featuring, and took care to sketch the various horn formations my six bulls in the climactic fight might have (pps. 44-45).

More rewarding in some ways, were the hours Vavra and I spent at the open holding pens in which the six bulls for a Sunday fight were held during the week prior to Sunday. There we conducted our own *sorteos* (sortings), making careful note of each bull, his social behavior with others, and his probable behavior when he entered the ring for the last, tremendous moments of his life. Such observation is the only way one can understand fighting bulls, and I have studied hundreds in this painstaking way. Two pages giving our complete notes on the bull fought by José Limeño at the 1961 *feria* in Seville have been retyped verbatim to fit one page and indicate how I worked (p. 46).

As I talked with Fulton and Vavra we evolved several further bits of information regarding the specific six bulls to be fought on the novel's final day in Toledo: a probable result of the sorting of the bulls (p. 47) and their allocation to each matador (this would be revised in 1991); and the plan of a typical Mexican provincial bullring, the kind with which John Fulton was amply familiar (p. 48).

The section closes with three random pages from the notebooks: the precise timing of the 'barbering' chicanery whereby a powerful bull is rendered almost harmless by shaving his horns (p.49); the street poem honoring the dead matador (p.50); and a jumbled page depicting my wrestling with names (p. 51).

Families In A Time Of Change

	ALTOMEC	AZTEC	PALAFOX	CLAY	LEAL
1504		1503 XUCHITL GIRL BORN	1502 TIMOTEO born		
1508	1505 Alicia born	1507 TEZ WIDOW DIES		1507 Celicia born	
1512					
1516					
1520	BORN XUCHITL 1519 -16 1503	1520 HMID NES 1527 Girl Born STRADLER BORN			
1524			1524 Soloman AM. MEXICO	1524 Alicia in Sevilla	
1528		1529 BAPTISM	1527 FORTRESS		
1532			1529 TIMOTEO venta Mexico 1530 IS .T.. Toledo		
1536					
1540		1540 Girl m.	Antonio 1538 Small mine		
1544			1544 GOBIERNO states		
1548			MINERAL		
1552					
1556					
1560					
1564					
1568					
1572		1570: Hall of house			
1576		1575 House Tile	575. House & Tile		
1580			TIMOTEO DIES ANT. DIES		
1584					
1588		GIRL DIES			
1592					
1596					
1600					

Families In Modern Times

GROG	LÓPEZ	GOMEZ	LEDESMA	RICARDO	BULL
1925					17
26					
27					
28	HIDING WITH GOMEZ	JUAN GOMEZ BORN (28)			
	LOPEZ	CRISTEROS COME		H.J.C. TO UNIV. & COLO.	
29	HIDING HIDELRL				
30					
31					
32			BURNING PIGHT	H.J.C MARRIED RACHEL MARTIN	
33					
34				RICARDO MARTIN CALDWELL BORN	
35					
36			FLIGHT TO FRANCE		
37			MEXICO POEMS		
38			SECOND-STRIK CHIL		
39		PIENTA - PALA		R.M.C. Prining Solve.	
40				H.J.C. Volunter Dec 8	

NORMAN CLAY

2. He is from Natxhez, Larenceville, Princetonx (ancestors P since 1764) Grandfather saw 30e in 1966

3. He saw Indian woman fifty years before...1910???

4. Father is Jpbn Clay. <u>The Pyramid and the Cathedral</u>

5. It is April, Fair 400 years old.

10. He had been in both World Wars (maybe father?)

11. Pyramid of Altomec existed 1400 years. Buitl 600s A.D. 1195 Altomecs conquer

12. Cathedral towers built 1640, ancestral Salamanca. Facade another Palafox bishop.

13. Arches of Palafox, another P Bichop 1726

27. In 1938 he was 29, so born in 1909, in 1961 he 52 old

VICTORIANO LEAL

167
A

Bernardo Leal [Cordan], killed by Miura bull in [bain of] Sevilla.
1860-1899

Anselmo Leal   JUSTO LEAL - PICED for { Joselito,
1892-1937   1894-   { Magias,
                                                     { Belmonte or [Pamona]
    } NOVILLERO
    } CIUDAD JUEZ
    } [Corrida] 1931   RICARDO   CHUCHO
                            1930   1937

    Leal y SUVEDA
← VICTORIANO y SUVEDA

1933 - Born

1947 - Novillero - RICARDO - CHUCHO   TOO INVOLVED

1952 - Alternativa

1886 [4 firm along] [days] -

───

Bernardo ~~Leal~~ y CORDAN   1868 - 1903

Came to Mexico in [crosfies] & [his Argentin]. Killed by [Pelote]
                                           [shock + son 3 devil]

ANSELMO [Good by]   JUSTO (VENENO)
         [2nd] [14 FEB 1935]
1901-1937 DIES [CONSUMPTION]   1896 -   WORKED FOR
         4 [Cab SCRIPTION]   FREG.
         [CAJON]   GRANERO
         [CLUSHUS]   ARMILLITA

VICTORIANO

    1933 -
    1946 - ~~PACIADORS~~ TIENTAS a [TALAITA]   MAR 1955 SPAIN
    1947 - C.J. [Novolata] SOBRESALIENTE JAN 1960 RETURNS
                           2 [NOVILLORS]
    1948 - MOST [FINITO CARE]

[Oct] 1952 - ARRUZA, MARTINEL. VICTORIANO [ALT]
                "   "   "   [CONFIRMS MEX]

Juan Gómez   BORN 1928   167 8

at home. 24 miles from [...] where his uncle worked.
Trienta at San Martin. Lopez Martin [...]. [...]
about. [...]. Tolido [...]: Bear belling. Chico. Féria
of 1944 [...]. That night at [...] y Tile. Banderillero.
Clipping. José [...] banderillero. [...] the
Novillada 1946. Chico [...]. Killed. Chico [...]. [...]   SENAQEKIB

Alternativa 1950.

1928 — Village [...] Palafox [...]. Mother & [...] Father
[...] in a skirmish in religious war. [...] lives with
them.

1942 — Trienta at Palafox. [...] to [...]
cows. [...], (Solorzano) Calesas. [...]. [...]
[...]. So [...]. He [...] brave [...] about
[...] immediately

1943 — Leon, [...], [...], Tacas. Chico Gonzaly   HONDURAS
Honduras

1944 — [...] Pr[...]. Féria [...]. Tremenda
[...] y bow. Take him out. That night bad.
Juan [...] Ramon CASTRO, CHICLES, gum chewer.

1944-46 on the road. ALTOS y JALISCO. PEPE LUIS VÁSQUEZ
NOVILLERO

1946 — RIO GRANDE ZAC SOBRESALIENTE - CALESERO y JUAN ESTRADA
CHICLES

TWO ENORMOUS QUOTES. "[...]" 15%, regular 10.

1947 — PICKS UP A LITTLE SPEED.

1948 — REAL BIG. RODRIGUEZ - CEPEDILLA - CORDOVA.

1958 — ALTERNATIVA SOLDADO PROCUNA - GAMEN

1951-60 — NOT SPAIN. BUT ALL FRONTIER.

Genealogy Of Our Bull

```
MARINERO
   ↓
1913   FIRST
   ↓
1923   SECOND
   ↓
1934   THIRD                              1933 NEW BULL  ←→ VACA  FROM  MARINERO
   ↓                                              ↓
1942   FOURTH  ←→  VACA  PIEDRAS NEGRAS          ↓
1944        FIFTH  BULL          1944      →MOTHER  OF  REINA
                          ↓
1947                  REINA
                          ↓
1951              RELAMPAGUITO          Bull put in unit 50 cows,
                          ↓              down to 30.
1955               TORTUGA
                          ↓
1956              SANGRE  AZUL
```

SANGRE AZUL

0-0	JAN.	1956?	BORN
1-0	JAN.	1957?	BRANDED
2-2	MAR.	1958?	TIENTA
3-11	DEC. FEB.	1959?	PICKED FOR IXHIQ
4-1	FEB.	1960?	KILLED
4-6	APR.	1960?	IXHIQ DESTINADO

33 rejected, designed.
Serial of 10% of prime opened
Finally 33 accepted to sober.

430 KILOS on the hoof.

44 gray   33 black

In Campo

15 bulls from same year. 2 different fathers. 44 starts mounting. Original manson taken to another corrida, so 44 tries 33.

But when 44 killed the new sobero cannot be put in unit the original 6. they would kill him.

Horn Types Of The Killers

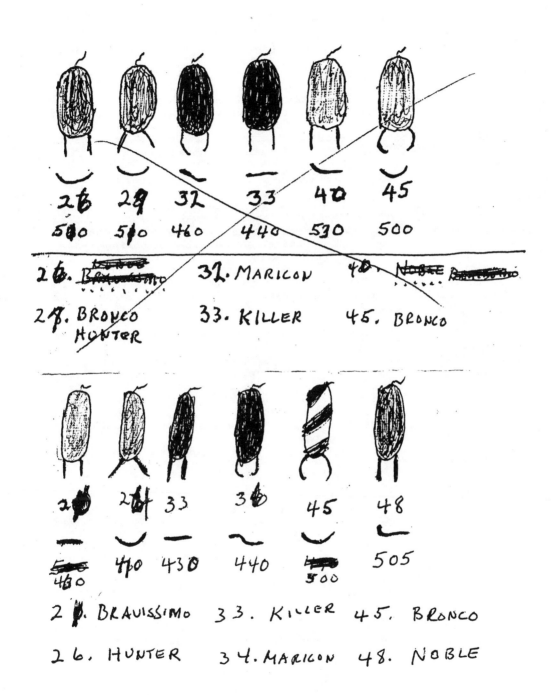

26.   29.   32.   33.   40.   45.
500   510   460   440   530   500

26. ~~Bronco~~   32. MARICON   40. ~~NOBLE~~ ~~Bronco~~

29. BRONCO HUNTER   33. KILLER   45. BRONCO

25.   26.   33.   36.   45.   48.
~~500~~ 460   470   430   440   ~~570~~ 500   505

25. BRAVISSIMO   33. KILLER   45. BRONCO

26. HUNTER   34. MARICON   48. NOBLE

Notes On A Great Bull

MICHENER'S APPRAISAL IN THE CORRAL

71. To be fought by José Limeno. 585 kilo est. Castano retinto [dark chestnut, almost black]. Best looking of the lot. Seems to avoid challenges from 72 and 75 by moving off. Avoids trouble from all quarters. Pairs with 121 for feeding and occasionally with 74. Very tranquil in the corrals and indifferent to men. Probably a fine bull. My choice because he will probably do very well with the horses.

MICHENER'S APPRAISAL DURING THE FIGHT

71. Limeno. 534 kilos. Fine entrance to left. Very quick, head high & rushing through capes. Chopped on boards. Varas very fine, recarga y empuja—very powerful and rushing charges. Knocked horses over three times, twice without taking varas. No quites—no dodging. Bull suave. Could take more pics, but adequately tired by his powerful attacks on the horses. 3 veronicas by matador, then wild running of the bull. 5 fine veronicas then turned his back to the bull in a corte. Bull feet up but workable.

Fine first banderillas, 2d pair not well done—bull defending itself valiantly and willing to run at anything. No 3d pair allowed by judge. Darkness approaching.

Bull slow to muleta, the small cape, then long charges but can also be fought close up. Kept nose tight in cloth but passes not much good, none of special emotion but all with courage. One fine series. Linkage faulty, bull tossed on the naturales passes and disengaged dangerously, but some work very close-in indeed. Estocada media—the sword thrusts half way, bull staggers long time, drops.

Great bull, not particularly well fought but bravely.

VAVRA's APPRAISAL

71. Limeno. Muy noble, suave. Very powerful in the varas. Probably the best bull of the entire feria. A miserable mistake that he did not have his ears cut. Taxidermist chose him as the best bull for mounting. Came out exactly as we had predicted in the corrals.

PROFESSIONAL CRITIC'S APPRAISAL

71. Baste decir, que el ultimo, con 534 , fue el mayor de la feria. Quiza, ademas, fue el mejor de la feria. (The last bull was not only the biggest of the feria but also the finest of the entire feria).

MICHENER'S VERDICT

"Did I pick 'em. Maybe the finest bull I've ever seen!"

Trickery In The Sorting

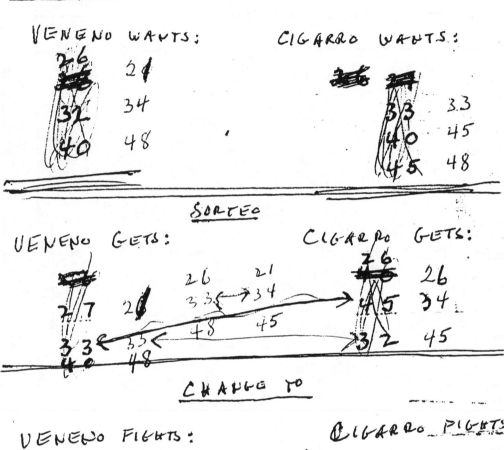

SORTEO

VENENO WANTS:

~~26~~ 21
34
~~40~~ 48

CIGARRO WANTS:

~~26~~ ~~21~~
33 · 33
40 · 45
45 · 48

SORTEO

VENENO GETS:

~~27~~ 2~~1~~   26   21
7 7   33 → 34
3 3   35 ← 48   45
40   48

CIGARRO GETS:

26 · 26
45 · 34
3 2 · 45

CHANGE TO

VENENO FIGHTS:

4 0   48
2 7   21
4 5   45

CIGARRO FIGHTS

3 7   34
26   26
3 3   33

Typical Mexican Bullring

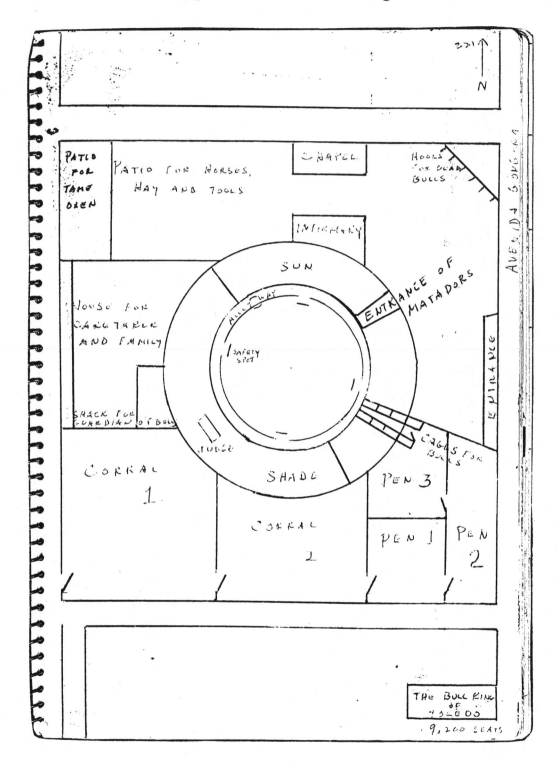

235A

PRECISE <u>TIMES</u> FOR THE BARBERS

4:30   to the Bullfight

6:30   Paquito dies

7:30   Story finished

8:00   Story filed

8:30   Cathedral

9:00   Museo

10:00   Dinner
         Program
11:30   Trip   CATACOMBS / MOORE MORE / ...

1:00   Crucifixion

1:15   Death

1:45   Carbide

2:00   Return

3:30   Plaza

4:30   Bulls arrive

5:30   Shaving done

6:00   Return to Hotel

6 – 7   Spanish Americans
8:30 – 9   Americans arrive (Get A.M.)

49

LAMENT FOR PAQUITO DE MONTEREY

211

He had an 8th grade education,
Could write and read the finest books.
He will be mourned by the entire population
For he was a young man of the most commanding looks.

Weep for Paquito!
His cup of tragedy is full,
Killed by Bonito,
That unfair and disgraceful bull.

His saintly mother lives in Monterey,
Where some of the world's finest glass is made.
Now the poor woman will weep night & day,
Because her son in dark earth must be laid.

Weep for Paquito!
Through all of Mexico's fair lands.
Killed by Bonito
On Toledo's blood-stained sands.

IXMIQ ———— OK

~VICTORIANO LEAL

VENENO
JOSE ROMERO
JUAN ~LEAL~ GRIS
    GOMEZ(2) LOPEZ
PEDRO, PABLO

MARK   DULANE
SCOTT   CABOT
WHIP   MARKER
ROLF
CORD

    MARK BINGHAM ?
MANNY LITWIN
HARRY LITWIN ←

LAKE DUCANE ~wife~
~FUSE~
    BESSIE GUNSTEENHOUN

SENAQERIB LEDESMA?
SENAQERIB ZOPILOTE

THE HOUSE OF TILE

TOLEDO ?

FIESTA

GRAL GRUG
VIERRA

THE HOUSE OF TILE

THE FIESTA OF IXMIQ

FOUNTAIN

DON TOMAS PALAFOX

NOCHE BUENA Beer
" Bock beer.
6 N. D. and it's h. Buenn
    for anybody. "

JUAN   GRIS   PEPU ORTEGA
JOSE   GOMEZ   CARMONA
PEDRO   LOPEZ
PABLO   •ROMERO
         PEREZ   CORTEZ
        •GIL   CORTES
         MOTO
         RIO   JOSE GOMEZ,
        •MOLINA   EL LOBO
         LOBO

TOLEDO   SEVILLE
RONDA

PAQUITO DE MONTERREY
PAQIRI   DC   "

Deciding the pairings of the bulls

III. THE GOSSAMER FILAMENT

Writing a novel is a perilous undertaking. To get it started is fairly easy, but to retain emotional, intellectual and psychological control as the chapters unfold is a demanding task. In the middle of the effort, doubts and confusion often arise and both confidence and forward motion are arrested and sometimes mortally wounded. Three times in my career I have stopped writing in midstream and subsequently abandoned the novel. Neither with *Mexico*, nor with a novel on the siege of Leningrad, nor with a novel on contemporary social relationships did I take refuge in the popular phrase 'writer's block,' for I have known that the fault lay not in some delicate psychological quirk in my mind but, rather, in the bald brutal consequence of my having lost control of the great enterprise. When asked about the demise of my grand hopes I have invariably said: 'It lost forward motion.' My careful use of the impersonal *It* betrays the fact that I was loath to blame myself for the disaster. Some outside agency was at fault. Actually, of course, the blockage was caused by my inability to keep the diverse strands in order, and especially to keep the ultimate target in sight and the channels to it clean and clearly defined.

A novel in process is especially vulnerable to this collapse. In fiction there is no inherent structure to the story being unfolded—it is free to go wherever the imagination or the experience of the writer elects. If she or he loses control of the grand design, the structure crumbles no matter how solidly the earlier foundations were built.

How much simpler is the problem of writing a non-fiction book for which the subject does have an inherent structure. If it is a biography of a politician, and the writer becomes temporarily confused, she or he will be supported by the inescapable historical facts that the subject of the biography did lose the election, did win four years later and then was brought to trial on charges that later proved spurious. The writer must deal with those subjects, and if the plan is to do so chronologically—not always the best way—there is an inherent plan but also an inherent obligation. If you presume to write a biography, your almost categorical imperative to cover a known body of material will keep you moving forward.

With a novel that is not the case. There is no obligatory structure or sequence to keep your mind in order. The outside world has no inherent understanding of what your novel should cover, and you are therefore not compelled to write in any preordained pattern. The novel goes where you want it to go, and if you lose your sense of direction, your novel founders and should, in many instances, be abandoned.

One of the strangest illustrations in world literature of the fact that a novel moves only as the writer decides is *Anna Karenina.* The heroine is the radiant, compelling focus of the tale, and commands our attention almost to the point of monopolization, but look at how Tolstoy ends her history. In the edition I have at hand Anna dies beneath the train on page 799, and there the story could end. But that was not Tolstoy's intention; he wanted to deal with much more than the suicide of his doomed heroine, and for an additional fifty-two pages, most of them rather tedious to the impatient reader, he makes us attend to the behavior of lesser characters like Sergey Ivanovich. And he never even shows them as they are affected by Anna's death; she is dead, dismissed and forgotten. These essentially irrelevant pages, insofar as Anna's story is concerned, form a curious appendage to a powerful novel. Few present-day writers would elect to use such a pattern, and if they did their editors would surely ask questions.

I have noticed that all dramatizations of this novel ignore the protracted conclusion, but a shrewd judge of fiction told me: 'Tolstoy was after something much bigger than Anna

Karenina in his novel. He was trying to portray a complete society and he felt compelled to add the rounded-out completion. Perhaps it was his attention to the more extensive portrait of Russian society that made his novel so powerful at its birth and so compelling ever since.' In other words, Tolstoy had a secure grasp of what he wanted to accomplish and the world has granted him that indulgence.

If in 1961 I had possessed a strong, clear vision of where I wanted to go, I would not have succumbed to the malaise that overtook me. Unfortunately I had not attained that clarity and, as a consequence, fumbled about so pitifully that I not only lost forward motion but began to retrograde. My reason for abandoning the novel at full tide was clear to me when it occurred— although up to now I have revealed the cause to no one—and is even more clear to me now. To explain I must speak of the relationship between a writer and the psychological world that controls him.

In the earliest days of my thinking about the miracle of writing I realized that the intellectual life of the writer is bound together by a tenuous silver cord whose strands are imagination, insight, intoxication with words, and a compulsion to share experience. Since writing came easily to me in those days I supposed that the cord binding these imperatives was a stout one, a rope actually, impervious to casual damage. And I wondered why, if some people I knew were determined to become writers, they did not simply get up early, sit down firmly at their typewriters and do it.

But as I learned more about writing and writers I saw clear evidence that some very gifted people with more abilities than mine were unable to get their lives and their talents into an orderly relationship. In those years I had access to many publishing houses of both books and magazines, and I introduced my gifted friends to editors who wanted to accept their manuscripts. In not a single instance were my friends able to discipline their abilities and turn in acceptable manuscripts; I succeeded in getting no one started on a career in writing books, even though they were demonstrably skilled in writing for newspapers or academic journals.* However, I must admit that their decision to quit trying was often forced by a wife's understandable nervousness when faced with eighteen months without family paychecks, as good a reason as any I know for abandoning a writing career.

At the same time that I was watching the apprehension of others, I was intensifying my own experiences in writing and publishing, and it became clear to me that the psychological, emotional and intellectual strands that bound me together did not constitute anything so strong and impermeable as a silver cord or rope. Far more tenuous than that, they were so fragile they could be damaged in a score of different ways: lack of attention to a book in the final stages of publication; a savage review; a realization that the parade of readers' tastes had almost imperceptibly passed one by, a change that left one alone on the curb as the pageant passed by; the inner suspicion that one's energies were flagging. From what I observed, it seemed that even one of these misadventures could often derail a career while a combination could be fatal. I was not nearly so indestructible as I had first imagined.

As a consequence of these sobering experiences I concluded that the life of the writer in all its manifestations was held together not by a stout silver cord but by a very fragile golden thread, the kind that held the sword suspended over the head of Damocles, susceptible to breakage at any moment. Since there are enough outside agencies determined to destroy that

---

* In later years I did help Oliver Statler, the distinguished writer on Japanese culture, find a publisher, and did the same with Neil Morgan, the California newspaper editor and social commentator, but I gave neither any assistance in actual writing, and with others I continued to fail. I did assist Robert Vavra, but only as a photographer; he learned writing on his own.

thread, a writer was out of his or her mind if he or she did anything voluntarily to weaken it, like excessive drinking or drugs. Keeping a writing career alive and functioning was a full time job, one requiring both constant attention and the courage to make difficult decisions.

It was in this frame of mind, aware at last of my own frailties, that I sat at my typewriter in Mexico City and drafted a unique document. My editors in New York seemed remote, and I sought both reassurance and direction. So I did what I had never done before and would surely never do again—I will smash my typewriter before I again allow it to transcribe such a stupid document. The job of a writer is to hammer out his own major decisions, not hide behind the counsel of others. The document included summaries of the progress of the novel to date, and sought advice as to how best to continue. By the time I mailed it, chapters 1-10 were already done, so this inquiry focused on what at this point were the seven chapters carrying the numbers 11 through 17.

A brief look at the excerpt from that letter on the following pages will remind the reader that chapters 11 through 15 would be brutally cut and regrouped, or dropped altogether, or reworked into something quite different. By now, in Chapter 9, my Texas girls whom I considered so important to the narrative had made a solid entrance. Such alterations demonstrated efficient planning, and in this case I was gratified with the results.

The deadly suggestion, the one that killed the manuscript in 1961, occurs in my proposal for Chapter 12 *The Operator,* and I invite careful attention to the actors in it. While thrashing around in an effort to find the appropriate conclusion to my narrative, one that would evolve naturally from things I'd witnessed in Mexico, I had attended a *tienta,* a festival testing of the two-year-old cows whose courage at that age, or lack of it, largely determines what courage, or cowardice, their male offspring will show. Hollywood stars like to slip down into

Chapter 8

The Picador

Friday night. This gives the history of the old picador, Veneno, who, with his two sons and the narrator, drive throug the night to intercept the bulls for the last corrida. They encounter the truck bringing the bulls in, but the watchmen from the ranch are alert, and nothing can be accomplished there. So the group trail the truck into Toledo, and after the bulls have been installed in the corral, quietly bring one after the other into a horn-cropping box, where the two young toreros skillfully shave down the horns, turn the points in, and release the animals with their defenses rather well neutralized. But before they can finish with all six, the guardian of the bulls suprises them, and they have to leave without having shaved down the horns of the last bull.

Chapter 9

The Americans

Saturday morning. At about ten the next morning the matador Fermin arrives in the Cadillac convertible of the blonde daughter of a Texas oil man, accompanied by two other girls, also Americans from Texas. An alaysis followsof the extra-ordinary group of American women who follow the bullfights and who latch onto matadors whenever possible. The two accompanying girls have not yet found theirs for this festival, but one recognizes the young Marine, Ricardo Martin, and through her the narrator gets the story of this young man, who has come to. Mexico determined to become a matador. His fight is with his father, a great amateur militarist who lives only to refight the Civil War, having been a jerkwater major in World War I on dep duty in New Jersey.

Chapter 10

The Saturday Bullfight

Without specifying the matadors, except the third, who is Fermin, this chapter details the unrelieved ugliness and brutality of a mediocre fight. The unbelievable behavior of the fans is studied and its effect upon the spectacle. The debacle drags on until the last bull, when Fermin, with a burst of fury, accomplishes at least an honorable attempt. The effect of this is seen upon the various Americans present.

Chapter 11

The Bull

A long chapter detailing the life of the bull whose horns were not clipped at the nocturnal shaving. The meaning of the fight, and the role of both the bull and his breeder, are developed. The chapter has several dramtic developments and ends with the unclipped bull in the corrals, waiting.

Chapter 12

The Operator

Sunday morning. The boy who brings the cables to the narrat also brings acable to the actors, from Sweden, advising them that the O'Neil festival is on and that they have the roles in Strange Interlude. They breathe easily and appear freely among the crowds, where the enthusiastic reception heartens them, but toward ten o'clock a car arrives from Mexico City with Roger Ramsay, Cabot's personal manager, and he has the good news that he has be able to arrange a mammoth production which will start Cabot in a Biblical

epic entitled JUDAS ISCARIOT. He explains how this is a natural for Cal
and that motivation research has studied movie-goers in thriteen cities
and that figures prove that the public would accept Cabot in the role of
Judas, and he would once more be back in business. The script has to be
adjusted here and there to take care of the television scandal, but actu
the latter is a plus value. Besides, there is a small role for Cabot's
wife. The latter fights this proposal and points out to Cabot that only
by starting over in Sweden, on the right course, can he truly recover.

Chapter 13

The Priest

This chapter takes a long look at the Catholic church in
Mexico, from a sympathetic angle, and explains how one prie
kept alive during the troubles and maintained both his san:
and his convictions. The relationship of the priest and :
bullfighter Juan Gomez is made clear.

Chapter 14

The Poet

Sunday morning. The young one-armed poet who appeared at 1
competition reenters the story with his version of the Chu
in Mexico, tells how he lost his arm, and explains, with tl
assistance of the local catacombs, the meaning of death.

Chpater 15

The Rooster

Sunday noon. The narrator takes his friends up to the old
mineral and recalls scenes from his childhood, especially t
role played in his life by The Rooster, a crippled matador
who served as watchman. At the sorting of the bulls for th
day's fight, he finds that The Rooster is now a functionary
at the ring. The choosing of the bulls takes place with Veneno fighting
to protect his matador from the one bull whose horns were not clipped.

Chapter 16

The Sunday Bullfight

The culminating fight sees Victoriano and Gomez each
fighting three bulls. The events are dramatic, leadi
to the fight of the fifth bull of the afternoon, the
one whose history we followed in Chapter 11. By lot
falls to Gomez and by innate trickery he gores Gomez.
Victoriano, instinctively coming to the rescue, is seriously caught by t
bull, but not killed, although it looked at first as if he would be. A
this point the young American Ricardo Maryin, jumps voluntarialy into th
ring and gives a series of fine passes, and is himself knocked down. Go
, his wound hastily taped shut, does final battle with the little bull.

Chapter 17

The House of Tile

Sunday evening after the fight. Victoriano, dangerously
wounded, is transported to Mexico City. The narrator appe
one last time to the critc for a fair report on the fight
gets turned down. The American girls each manage to find
bullfighter for the night. The narrator, the critic, Rica
Martin and Cord Cabot's wife. The actor has gone back to Hollywood to st
in the sleazy production of JUDAS ISCARIOT, but his wife is determined t
go on to Sweden to rebuild. The talk focuses on what young Martin will
to do to become a real bullfighter. Cabot's wife wants to know what it
will cost in money, and the critic explains in brutal clarity. The actr
offers to put up the money, "because I want to see one man do what he kn
ought to be done." The festival is ending.

In the passageway

northern Mexico to attend *tientas*, and they are enthusiastically welcomed by the ranchers, for the male stars are usually willing to try their luck with the fighting cows and some of the young starlets show spectacular bravery in holding one end of a rather small cape while a practiced matador holds the other some four feet away from her. In tandem, separated from each other as far as the cape permits, they walk slowly toward the cow until the animal charges like a thunderbolt. Standing firm, the matador and the starlet allow the cow to charge furiously between them. It's an exciting moment.

At the *tienta* I attended there was a male star of excellent reputation who was accompanied by a starlet he was wooing, and they behaved with great flair, entering into the festivities as if they were practiced hands with the tumultuous cows. Watching them, I visualized another even more famous actor I had known in Hollywood briefly and his actress wife. I doubt if either of them had ever attended a *tienta* in Mexico, but in my imagination they did and I saw good reason why they might be participating in the weekend fiesta about which I was writing. So with excitement and enthusiasm I admitted them into my outline, and when I drafted their probable behavior into my plan I was satisfied that I had come upon the sensible conclusion to my imaginary fiesta and also my novel.

I typed out the entire scenario as I envisaged it and mailed it off to New York for my editors' reactions. A copy found its way into the hands of my good friend, Bennett Cerf, president of Random House, and when I returned to New York he sought me out: 'Jim, I think you already have a strong novel, one that's sure to be a big success. Why do you feel you have to schmaltz it up with Hollywood types who sound like Tony Curtis and Janet Leigh?'

The question stunned me. Bennett had told me about his unfortunate marriage to a Hollywood star, and although he had never spoken a word against her, he did betray the fact that he held her Hollywood counselors largely responsible for the breakup of his marriage. I thought I understood why he might not want me to introduce Hollywood personalities into my narrative, but they nevertheless were legitimate participants in a *feria*, as I had seen on three different occasions. This was no spurious invention on my part.

Furthermore, I had a solid regard for the business-like acting of Tony Curtis, whose 1959 appearance with Jack Lemmon in Marilyn Monroe's *Some Like It Hot* was a masterpiece of one actor's submerging himself in the persona of another. I had also liked him as the sleazy publicity agent in Burt Lancaster's *Sweet Smell of Success*, where his performance was controlled, beautifully observed and properly tragic. Miss Leigh I did not know, but her 1960 performance in Hitchcock's *Psycho*, in which she marvelously depicted a young embezzler, proved that she could accept direction and give a touching performance of a young woman about to be murdered by Norman Bates.

To me they were not a contemptible nor unproductive pair, but the scorn with which Cerf dismissed their prototypes had a shocking effect on me. If I tried to depict my Hollywood couple at the fiesta in the dispassionate, neutral terms which I intended, would they come off as a pair to be dismissed as unreal, or what was worse, not worthy of serious attention?

I liked Cerf, respected his judgment on books, and apart from his loud support of the New York Yankees ball club, that collection of masters who year after year humbled my three favorites, the Phillies, the Boston Red Sox and the Brooklyn Dodgers, I found him delightful to be with. I remembered him warmly for two of his many masterly performances. Early on, when initiating me into his publishing company where he would help me to an unbroken chain of good fortune, he advised me: 'Jim, whenever you go into a strange town, stop at the bookstore. Tell the owner and especially the clerks how much you appreciate their support. Because they're the ones who'll keep you alive.'

I said, 'Now I see why the professionals are so fond of you. The only cost of courtesy is a little time.'

'It isn't as simple as that. Because if they see you're really interested in books they'll ask you to autograph one or two, for their special customers. Always do it. In fact, autograph all the books of yours they have. Because then they can't ship the unsold copies back to us for a refund.'

His other master stroke came when he published an autobiography by a man in Canada who'd had an amazing series of adventures on the various World War II battlefronts of Europe. The author had been a self-effacing hero who refused to acknowledge the extreme dangers he faced during his exploits. Entitled *The Man Who Wouldn't Talk*, the book was what they call 'a great read' and attracted so much attention that it became a bestseller.

But rumors began to reach New York casting doubt on the authenticity of the yarn. Although the author was a likable fellow, a great raconteur and a devotee of books on military subjects, a Canadian newspaperman discovered that he had never been stationed outside of Canada or England during the war and had composed his book in an exercise of what-might-have-been.

A scandal erupted, making Random House look rather silly for having been deceived by the author and for having circulated a fraud. Many of us wondered how Cerf would handle this debacle, and we were both amused and relieved when he sent brief telegrams to booksellers: 'Recommend you shift *The Man Who Wouldn't Talk* from non-fiction to fiction. Its new title is *The Man Who Talked Too Much*.' Nationwide laughter supplanted criticism and sales increased five-fold, an example of Cerf's creative publishing.

In our long relationship Cerf and I never became intimate buddies—our styles were too antithetical—but we did respect each other, and in 1961 when I was more impressionable than now, his comments ridiculing my proposed introduction of the

Hollywood types into my novel quite disarmed me. I wasted so much time trying to justify my suggestion artistically, and even more time seeking a better story line if I discarded this one, that I lost control of my narrative.

In a conversation that could not have lasted more than six minutes, Bennett Cerf, my own publisher, had destroyed any chance I might have had of finishing my novel in timely form. I hasten to add that his criticism was correct; it was a carefully considered judgment and one that I would recognize as meritorious and adopt years later when I returned to the manuscript. Prototypes of Tony Curtis and Janet Leigh, admirable as they might be, had no place in this book, and to try to force them in would have trivialized the story. I think I knew at the time that Cerf was right, that his judgment was superior to mine, but the light-hearted manner in which he delivered it, and my insecure condition when I received it, killed my Mexico experiment as completely as if a ten-ton charge of TNT had struck it.

In a kind of stupor I put the manuscript aside, interring it among my papers as a dead item. I wrote not another word, buried the affair in my consciousness, and erased all traces of it. Back in Pennsylvania I packed the many pages of the manuscript and its three notebooks into a neat box, for I like to be careful of even dead copy, and prepared everything for shipment to the Library of Congress, which had been collecting my papers for some years. *Mexico* was dead and respectfully buried. I had regrets but no recriminations; I'd made a major effort over three years and had failed. Time to get on with some new assignment.

After disposing of the corpse and giving it decent burial, I paused to contemplate the nature of writing fiction, and I saw that an author's emotional-creative-productive axis was linked together not by either a silver cord or a golden thread but by a gossamer filament, an entity so fragile that even a gust of untimely cold wind could break it into temporary fragments, while a brutal assault could destroy it completely, often past any chance of reassembly. Literary history contained numerous examples of writers who were derailed by criticism. John Keats was so devastated that his death seems to have been hastened; Thomas Hardy retreated into poetry after being rebuked for the moral improprieties of his great novels; and several fine American writers, who did first-rate but unrecognized first novels, lived on in obscurity until their books were belatedly honored. Both ordinary talent and rare genius can be nipped in the bud by criticism.

Such reflection led me to the conclusion that the gossamer filament which holds the artistic life together is so delicate that it hardly bears analysis. It is as fragile as the spinal column, just as susceptible to permanent damage, and just as necessary to continued activity. It is nebulous, of different weight and composition in all men and women, and must be shielded carefully if one hopes to survive as an artist.

After that disastrous experience of exchanging ideas and plans with Bennett Cerf—he completely right, I wrong—I adopted a policy of brutal clarity and ease of enforcement. I would consult with no one about my plans. I would not announce what ideas I was contemplating. I would allow no one to read anything I'd written until it was completed. And while my highly skilled assistants, an immortal breed as most writers learn, worked on their typewriters or word processors— the only people who knew what I was doing—I neither invited nor relished their comments on the manuscript. And it is a demonstrable fact that on many occasions neither my agent nor my publisher has known what I was working on until I delivered a completed manuscript into their hands. I have not even discussed with my wife the precise kind of writing I was doing, for I sought guidance from no one; but she was the first to read the finished work. As the former editor of a magazine she was skilled as a proof reader.

I adopted this rigorous policy in self-defense, for I had learned through three abortive attempts at finishing a novel—

this one on Mexico, the one on the siege of Leningrad, and the one on contemporary social relationships, each of which I had to abandon in mid-flight—that I must permit nothing to imperil my forward progress. I had not suffered writer's block; I had experienced writer's annihilation. The gossamer filament was like the bejeweled cobweb that glistens with dew in early morning; it could be obliterated by one blast of sunlight, and I must not allow this to happen again.

Of course, once I have a manuscript completed to my early satisfaction, I distribute relevant chapters, and sometimes the whole, to experts in the subject matter being treated in hopes that they might help me avoid gross error, and they do. I have been significantly assisted by the intelligent people I have consulted, and am indebted to them for their comments. Only after the novel is safely drafted and completed to the best of my ability, however, do I ask my peers and my editors for counsel—usually paying the former for their adverse criticism.

The protection of one's personal source of power and one's integrity as an individualized spokesman is vital to a writing career. For that reason I do not read criticism of my work after it is published. I cannot profit from favorable reports; the work is already done. And I dare not allow unfavorable reviews to alter my perception of my work or in any way modify what I might want to do in the future. The preservation of that gossamer filament which holds my personality, my perceptions and my performance together so delicately has become a major obligation in my life.

The death of my Mexican novel thus became the birth of the philosophy that has sustained me.

IV. LAZARUS

In the autumn of 1961 when I acknowledged that my novel about a fiesta in Mexico had died a strangling death and boxed it for burial in the Library of Congress, I placed the coffin, properly addressed, on the table where my wife and I assembled the various bits of mail that had to be taken to the post office or picked up by the forwarding agent who handled the larger packages. I remember with clarity calling the shipper in Doylestown: 'I have another package for Washington. Please pick it up as usual and send me the bill.' They said they'd drop by on their afternoon run. They did, and the manuscript was gone with no regret on my part, disappointment that a project which had started so promisingly had ended in failure, but no recrimination.

Why, if the project was dead, did I take such pains to collect and deposit materials involved in its writing? The Library of Congress had, for several decades, operated a system whereby each year it gathered written materials that showed how ordinary citizens made their living. In the 1940s, long before anyone had heard of me, they picked my name out of a hat as illustrative of people working in the publishing industry, invited me to serve as one of their guinea pigs, and I agreed. I was therefore obligated to send them the manuscript, for they were as interested in my failures as in my successes. I did not force it upon them, but I was relieved to have it off my hands and in safe keeping, should someone at a future date be interested in how writing projects sometimes collapsed.

During the three decades that followed, 1961-91, numerous interested persons who had been aware of my work on Mexico asked me what the chances were for my reviving the effort, for they remembered it as a solid potential book. Bennett

Cerf, before he died, questioned me repeatedly. He feared we had lost a good book, and I dared not explain the role he had played in its abandonment.

Albert Erskine, my long-time editor at Random House, also asked numerous times, for he felt sure the project could be revived. Disappointed whenever I said the novel was dead and properly buried in the Library of Congress, he recommended that it be retrieved and reworked. I said I regretted that this could not be done, for when I deposited any of my papers it was with the understanding that they would not be opened until twenty-five years after my death. The partial book was safely and securely interred and was not available . . . to me or anyone else.

My agent Helen Strauss, who had skimmed the first ten chapters, was convinced that they formed two-thirds of a book almost completed, and she implored me to go to Washington and retrieve it. Her interest was both personal and professional; my subsequent books had been well received and she felt that the public would be interested in reading about my reactions to life in Mexico. Since she would receive ten percent of any sales, she wanted the book to be circulated and was distressed when I said it was locked away forever.

A Washington D.C. newsman, Harvey Hagman, interviewed me from time to time, always asking about the Mexico project and always I said: 'It lost forward motion and I put the idea to rest.'

In the 1980s my office coordinator and personal assistant, John Kings, having heard from various people about the manuscript, asked permission to work with the Library of Congress experts in an effort to retrieve it. I finally agreed to allow a search through the mass of my papers, a task in which John was aided by Dr. Alice Birney, American Literature Specialist in the Manuscript Division of the Library of Congress. When she came up with no clues whatever, she began to wonder whether it had ever arrived at the Library.

The most urgent advocate of finding the papers was my wife Mari, for she had been with me in Mexico and Spain when I worked on the project. She remembered the Hotel Cortés as one of the most congenial we had ever occupied, and our trips into the countryside to study the bulls had been an exciting adventure for a young married woman. Since she felt a part of the Mexican adventure she wanted to see the book in print. I cannot count the number of times she said: 'You've got to find it. If they don't want to search for it, I'll go to Washington. I was an editor for the American Library Association and they'll give me privileges.' I said that if the people trained to do such work had not found the big bundle of manuscript, there was little chance that an outsider could.

'Then where is it?'

'I suppose it must have been either lost or thrown out.'

'Are you sure you sent it?'

'Positive. My cousin Virginia even saw me pack the photographs.' But the papers could not be found.

At this point a new, dynamic force entered the picture. When Helen Strauss voluntarily retired from the William Morris Agency for an executive job in Hollywood, her place as my agent devolved upon her young assistant, Owen Laster, with whom I would have a long and fruitful association. One day, as he studied the various contracts governing his agency's relations with me, he found to his amazement that a now-very-old contract still existed between Random House and me for the publication of a novel centering on a three-day bullfight fiesta in an imaginary Mexican city. At the time the contract was written the work was called *Festival.*

When he read the legal papers he sprang into action, for if the manuscript could be finished he would have an unexpected ready-made novel at a time when my books were doing well. With adequate proof that the manuscript existed, and driven by a determination to find it, he asked me repeatedly over a period of many years: 'Jim, where could that Mexico manuscript be?' As one possibility after another was dismissed, I lost interest in the search, but he did not.

Joining forces with John Kings, who also believed the manuscript might somehow be recovered, Laster decided to start fresh and probe all likelihoods. To confirm that I had sent the papers to Washington, they consulted with my cousin, Virginia Trumbull of Salisbury, Maryland, who had been living with us when I shipped the package and she told them: 'Yes, I remember the affair, primarily because Jim had included in the shipment a large album of family photogaphs reaching back nearly a hundred years.'

'Can you verify that the pages of the novel were also in the package?'

'Jim said they were, and the size would indicate that.'

'Are you satisfied that the package was delivered to the forwarding agent?'

'It was certainly ready for him.' She remembered the photographs; that they had been with the manuscript there could be no doubt, and she supposed that they too had been lost in the Library.

That was how things stood in the spring of 1991 when Laster came to Austin, Texas, to work with me on a nagging publishing problem. At a social dinner with Kings and me he once more raised the question of this unfulfilled contract: 'I think we ought to make a comprehensive effort to find this thing,' and Kings replied: 'Coincidence! Random House has asked me to supply family photographs for Jim's book of memoirs, and I have none. But it occurred to me that if Virginia Trumbull could find that large batch of photos Jim said he mailed to the Library, I might find all I need.'

'What are you doing about it?'

'I've asked her to wrack her brain as to where the photos might be, and she told me: "I wonder if the package could have been treated as if someone had sent it *to* Jim, rather than Jim's sending it out to someone else?" She is willing to drive back to

Pennsylvania and fine-tooth the place to see if just maybe . . . .'

I had not been aware of this mission and said: 'Futile. But she's a stubborn woman, so if she wants to go, encourage her!' The result of her trip, which I dismissed as forlorn, is described in her report to me:

When John Kings called me about the photographs I first thought of the old red tin box in which photographs were kept in the attic at 96 Harvey Avenue. This box was about six inches deep by twelve long and about eight wide. Then later I recalled bringing you a box of assorted photographs in a white letter-sized box or slightly larger.

As John kept calling and asking for more details about the pictures it seemed to me that since the Library could not locate them, they must still be at your house in Pipersville and at that time I suggested it might be helpful if I went to see what I could find since Mari and I have a better notion of what the house contains than anyone else.

When John called to ask if I would undertake the search, I began to turn over in my mind where to look. When Pat and I had first moved onto the hill, I remember Mari showing us a box in the study off the kitchen and remarking that it held material being accumulated for shipment to the Library of Congress. Later the material was moved to the Gallery, but it seemed reasonable to start my search in the small study. . . .

Your study was very tidy and it was obvious there was nothing on the bookshelves there so I started on the file cabinets. The small file cabinet under the windowshelf yielded nothing. . . .The main file cabinet next to the window also had nothing, but finally in the third drawer from the top of the second file cabinet there was the photograph album lying in solitary splendor. I was really pleased and relieved to

Plaza manager

Matador's manager

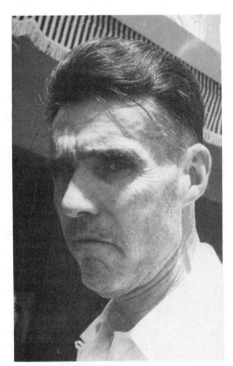

Plaza workman

Ganadero

My notebooks contained these photographs of men whose

Rancher

Picador

Banderillero

Péon de Confianza

faces reflect the color and drama of the bullfight.

find it as I had felt sure the photos were somewhere
in that end of the house.

I first learned the result of her amazing find one Monday
morning as Kings and I were driving to work at The University
of Texas: 'Virginia Trumbull called to say that she had gone to
your old house on the hill and found the packet of photographs
we were seeking.'

'That's wonderful! Do they show all members of the
family?'

'That and a lot more. I haven't seen them, of course. She's
mailing them. But I judge from her description that we have
everything we need.'

I was delighted by this reassuring news, for it meant that
my book of memoirs would be properly fleshed out with
photographs of the important characters in the story, but then
he stunned me with further information from Virginia: 'As she
was about to leave the hill, she happened to look in a remote
corner of a storage area, and there she found a box with a huge
amount of material from the Mexican novel.'

'What was in the box?'

'She said she didn't want to disturb it, so she couldn't tell
me. But she said it was copious. It's already in the mail.'

Because such a resurrection must seem improbable, I had
better allow Virginia to explain how it happened:

> I moved to the other side of the room and started on
> the shelves which held some boxes. I had to get the
> little stepladder from your closet to reach the shelves
> and had lifted down two boxes of papers when I
> noticed a cardboard box with "Mexico" written on
> the side.

> The top papers in the box concerned the Constitu-
> tional Convention to which you were a delegate, and
> beneath that were a group of papers in strong clips:
> Chapter One, etc., then a notebook with

> photographs of Mexican scenes, chiefly churches, as
> I recall, and then more papers in clips. Just a glance
> showed that this was the missing book! What a
> surprise and pleasure that was!

Her report left me speculating on the extent of the two caches
she had found, but two days later her big package arrived, in
two sections as I recall. John Kings had his photos, and
remarkably clear and clean they were, dating back to the 1860s,
and I had my manuscript. When I opened the box I found my
original typing of the first ten chapters, my secretary's clean
retyping in condition ready for the editors, two fat notebooks
containing the results of all my work in Mexico and Spain, a
third notebook crammed with well over a hundred photos I'd
taken of the bullfight milieu in both countries, and a mass of
inchoate material of great interest that had not yet been placed
in notebooks. It was a treasure that contained everything I
remembered, everything I needed to complete the remaining
chapters. It was an invitation to start work. It was a miracle.

But it was not that simple because, as always, I was deeply
involved in numerous other projects, Although I try never to
work on more than one original composition at a time, I had
several completed manuscripts that were more or less ready for
publication. To add to the complexity, our family doctor, a
man we trusted and with good reason, told my wife: 'Since some
years ago you had a cancerous breast removal, you'd be wise to
have a careful mammography of your other breast,' and we
agreed. The X-ray was taken. A lump was found. A biopsy
proved that it too was cancerous, and as a husband I observed
the mental hell that women are put through, not only when a
breast shows an advanced cancer but even when a mere spot
appears. This time my wife had the simplest cancer a woman
could have, and both she and I were eager to have it excised.

To perform this simple medical routine we had to consult
eight different specialists: family doctor, cancer specialist,
radiologist, interpreter of the radiogram, doctor who treated the

first cancer (my wife did not have to consult the doctors of ten years past, but she wanted to), radiologist who applied radiation for the first time, and the surgeon who would do the operating. To help us decide which of the four radically different procedures to adopt, an oncologist spent almost two hours with us doing nothing but laying out our options: first, a lumpectomy which attacks only the lump or a more comprehensive cutting; second, heavy radiation to follow every possible avenue of metastasis or light radiation of the site; third, chemotherapy to knock out vagrant cancer cells after the operation; or fourth, reliance upon a new drug which showed promise in killing off dangerous cells. The surgeon said: 'Take the heavy radiation.' The radiologist said: 'With a small lump I'd not take the radiation.' When Mari asked each man: 'What would you do if it were your own wife?' their answers were equally consistent: 'Heavy radiation.' 'No radiation.' 'Chemotherapy!' 'No chemotherapy!'

And when we asked the oncologist at the conclusion of his excellent explanation: 'So what should we do?' he said: 'You have to make up your own mind. But if you take every precaution, we find you'll have about a ninety-seven percent chance of complete cure.' He did not have to tell me that if you did nothing the prognosis was grim. For I had followed the cases of three women younger than my wife who had refused any mutilation of their breasts, and in due course we had buried each of them, prematurely.

In this crucial moment of our lives, no doctor was willing to state authoritatively: 'Do this' or 'Do that.' And when we looked into the national statistics we found that the recommended procedure for this plague against women depended upon which part of the country you lived in: in one region it's all lumpectomies; in other it's radical cutting; in another there is great reliance upon radiation; in another it's chemotherapy. The treatment of breast cancer is in one hell of a mess because male doctors who determine priorities in medical research and cure have not given priority to this plague. We do have, however, one encouraging practical conclusion: 'If the patient adopts all the alternatives, the survival rate is ninety-seven percent,' and those are heartening odds.

So on the precise day my long-lost manuscript arrived, our family concluded that Mari would go the full routine and we'd pray this second mastectomy would prove as successful and healing as the first. We would have to remain in blazing Texas instead of emigrating to cool Maine, but for me that simplified things. I would stay home and support my wife in every possible way and in my free time work on the resurrected notebooks, the outlines, and the improvements intimated by the annotations. Mari would be in the radiation room daily for six weeks, and I would be at my typewriter fourteen and fifteen hours a day. My work would prove therapeutic for both of us—Mari could be sure I wasn't fretting myself into despair, while I could be sure that she was doing the right thing.

When I opened the manuscript on the day Mari had her operation, I found an orderly array of past accomplishment, notes and ideas for future work, and a partial design for the seven remaining chapters. To attack the problem rationally I first read the ten existing chapters, and I must confess that in doing so I saw why Bennett Cerf, Albert Erskine and Helen Strauss had high regard for them. Unfinished and unpolished they were, but they were real writing about real characters and significant historical events. They formed a solid base on which to build further, although I could see a few places where my thinking had changed so sharply that revisions would be necessary.

Satisfied that the work done years ago was still vital, I combed the notebooks for pages on which the remainder of the book had been outlined, and when I had codified the tentative directives of the numerous outlines and arranged them on one page, it was clear, as I have said earlier, that a good deal of cleaning up had to be done.

I therefore analyzed each of my ideas, however fugitive,

and in a ruthless process of elimination and consolidation and devising new chapters, I came up with this proposal for the conclusion and, with the eventual addition of a new chapter entitled *On the Terrace*, it remained the directive.

JAM 1991

1. Cactus & Maguey
2. The Spaniard
3. The Rancher
4. The Indian
5. Indian Ancestors
6. The Critic
7. Bullfight #1
8. Meaning of Death
9. The Barbers
10. Spanish Ancestors
11. The Americans
12. Bullfight #2
13. By Torchlight
14. American Ancestors
15. The Sorteo
16. Bullfight #3
17. House of Tile

On 30 June 1991 I did with the new writing project what I had learned to do with any major task: I went to my typewriter and drafted the ideas which appear in the upper right-hand corner of the following page. I had committed myself to go forward with the project, but I did not immediately attempt to identify or outline the difficult remaining chapters. Instead, I studied my past efforts as outlined in the previous pages, and the next morning I was prepared to draft the ending to the manuscript. In the upper left-hand corner I stated my intentions, and on the remainder of the page I tried to give a succinct précis for each of the seven fugitive chapters. My Texas girls were solidly ensconced in Chapter 11. I had the remaining chapters in their proper order except that *The Barbers* and *Spanish Ancestors* would change position and later, when it came time to write Chapter 13 *By Torchlight*, I saw that it had to come after my Chapter 14 *American Ancestors*, since the midnight drama had to rely upon information and activities in the *American Ancestors* chapter. Final correction was easily made and I had a workable template, one which served admirably.

1 July 1991

A full week of thought about the manuscript
has left me with some solid ideas about it
but not so weighty decusions about what I as
a writer ought to do next. Iam engulfed with
projects, manuscripts everywhere, things I
k('t desire to do, but none exceeds the excitement I feel when I read these wonderful
chapters. They deserve to be finished, and I
have plotted a way to do this as shown in the
outlines below. I have a shuliering concept
for every chapter, ideas that go back a third
of a century, and are as vital today as when
I first generated them. I've dropped I've dropped
two of the major chaoters, having been unable
to deduce what they represented; the others
are boiling and ready to go. Succinctly: I can
find the imagination and desire to finish off
the book, but I'm bewildered as to how tomhow
to set aside the concentrated time it will
take to do it. As of this morning I am still
unclear as to priorities and possibilities,
but that merely means: 'Do more work, clear

30 June 1991

For exactly a week I've been pondering how to react to
the miraculous finding of the Mexican novel. Ten lon
chapters arrived in flawless print-out and I8ve had a
remarkable experience in reading them and renewing ac
aintance with a wonderful group of characters, settin
and incidents. I vould do little to improve upon the
ten. I also have with the chapters six different set
of notes as to how the book was to be finished off; so
give me nine additional chapters; some seven; and one
a super-comprehensive twenty three. At first glance
decided that I was not competent to pick up the golde
read that I had severed, but as I worked in the man
script, and especially the 246 pages of notes---most
them useless or indecipherable, I caught sudden insig
plus some really wonderfiul imaginings, and very slow
ly I could piece together what the chapters intended
and knit into a comprehensible whole the fragments of
ideas. It can be done. The story has crept bacl to
life, and all I need now is the 150 scheduled pages..
I had specified how many pages to each missing chapte
...that the plan calls for. That can be done. It can

11. The Americans: The three college girls
from Texas come roaring into town to find
themselves some bullfighters. They have letters
of intriduction to Norman Clay and hope that he
will be able to make introductions. Mrs. Evans
knows the parents of the lead girl (name unknown
to me at present) and she astiubds her fellow
t(ists from Oklahoma by abetting the girls,
who have been awed by the death of Paquito that
ternoon, but contacts are made.

12. The Saturday Fight: I planned originally
for two real bullfighers and an imaginary: Procuna
Rodriguez, and Fermin, but xmxm later I changed
to all imaginary, but bow I want to pay tribute
to my dear friend Calesero with whom I went to
many fights in Mexico. But Fermin remaims, The
outline of the fight has been well designed in
my notes from 1960 and I shall follow them. One
of the Texas girls grabs hold of Fermon, the
other takes one of the Leal peones. (227)

13. By Torchlight: I could not decipher this at
first and abandoned itk for the notes were too
fragmentary. But as they coalesced I became en-
chanted with the scene, the music, the words, the
interplays. The one-armed Altomec poet reads his
text for a powerful pageant. the critic approves,
Mrs. Evans is excited by the characters the poet
presents. And the Texas girl takes Victoriano to
bed.

14. American Ancestors: I've always had a crystal
ght into Norman Clay...Virginia (not Natchez
now/,...his grandfather at Cold Harbor, cannot a-
b' the horror of Grant's sucidal charges (sui-
c. s for the soldiers, not Grant) and in revolting
disgust he and nine of his friends decide to quit
the States and take residence in Mexico, as many
did. The marriage, the mineral, the fortune, the
1915-1917 war, the church, the army, the loss.

15. The Sorteo: Picking the bulls for the climactic
Sunday fight. This occurs at high noon Sunday, and
Mrs, Evans is invited by the critic to participate
She watches the chicanery as the critic explains i
amd sees how Veneno does everything possible to pro
tect his son Victoriano. Attention is focused on
the fine bull # 43, whose horns have not been shave
do as to make him less capable of defending himself
He is a powerful creature and the citic predicts th
he'll give a good account of h mself. Veneno sees t
43 dies not fall to his nephew (his son) and Mrs.
Evasn asks Clay what he's going to photograph of th
fight, since t e murder he sought has taken place

16. The Sunday Fight: A group of bullfighters wi
whom I traveked in Mexico helped me to devise the a
atgies for this important fight, and when I saw my n
I gloated, for there they were as I had written the
from dictation years ago. It is a mano-a-mano, tha
is, only two matadors, which makes for some interes
ing byplay in the banderillas, because it is now mo
difficult to prevent your opponent from outshining
you with your own bull. The fight proceeds accordin
to the script done years ago, Martin espontaneo.

17. The House of Tile: I8ve oscillated a score
times on the title for this chapter, always betw
the one given and a plain Mrs. Evans. I see it
the tremendously mournfuo end to fiestas that I
witnessed in Pamplona, the heart wrenching suspicion tha t the fiendships would never be renewe
that one might never again find the time or the
money to particopate in the wild grandeur of the
festival, the songs no more, the dinners at the
House of Tile, the intricacues of the bull world.
the camaraderie, the passage of time dreadful, i
herent shabbiness of the festival, whether i Ri
Seville, Trinidad or New Orleans. Norman Clay
remembers the english music teacher who had come
to Pamplona years ago 'Pobre de mi' echoes as he
goes to speak with the statue of his grandfather.

Faced by the demanding task of recapturing the mood in which I had worked on the first ten chapters in order to finish the last seven, I was aided by two unusual conditions: since Mari was in the hospital I had no car and had to stay home; and thoughtful neighbors saw to it that I had food. Even when my wife came home to start her heavy radiation, other neighbors ferried her to and from the hospital laboratory. Again this left me alone at home for the twenty-eight days it took for her to complete her treatments. Fortunately the radiation seemed to halt the cancer, so that when she came home mended she found me deep into my work, and her revived spirits helped me to complete it.

It seemed at times that Mari and I were back in Mexico City, making our expeditions into the countryside, and to Guanajuato, the scene of my imaginary city of Toledo. I was with the matadors I had known in those days, with the ranchers at whose *tientas* I had tried to cape the fierce young cows without success. The girls from Hollywood were braver and better than I. And the narcotic wonder of the three-day *feria* in Matador Calesero's hometown came back in magical force. There were the *mariachis* I had loved, the *flamenco* dancers who had charmed me, the museum, the catacombs with ranks of standing mummies all in colonial costume, and in the distance the pyramid, while near at hand the ominous silver mine dipped deep into the earth. Mari and I were again in the old Hotel Cortés and the decades vanished, leaving me with the burgeoning enthusiasm I had known in those days of dedication.

What did I accomplish during my period of isolation? The next three illustrations, the last ones to be reproduced from either my 1961 notebooks or my 1991 study, show what I tried to accomplish. The most important task, upon which all else depended, was straightening out my *American Ancestors,* and the work-page shown on the following page served as a faithful though jumbled guide. Since the chapter grew into a novella of its own, one hundred and sixty pages of freighted manuscript,

13. AMERICAN ANCESTORS

30 June 199?   IV-12

NORMAN CLAY 1909-5? in 1961

Jubal Clay – ?
- Born 1825   3
- Mexico 1847   22
- Cold Harbor 1864   39
- Mexico 1866 – 41
- Marries 1850 – 49 NEWFIELDS
- Dies 1838   65 87
  1910   1910 ?

Mexican War
- March 1847   Invested Vera Cruz
- March 27   Took Ulua
- April 8   March to Interior
- May 15   Puebla
- Sept. 12-13 Chapultepec
- Sept 14   Entered Mexico City

John Clay
- Born 1882
- DIES 1945

Norman Clay
- Born 1909

WINFIELD SCOTT 1786-1866
JUBAL EARLY 1816-1894
LEW WALLACE 1827-1905
BEN HUR 1880

COLD HARBOR
31 MAY 1864   115
12 June 1864
5000 CH PLIFFIELD
14000 NORTH-ILD

372 LEE'S ARMY 56,000 men
373 GRANT'S ARMY 65,000

PINCELADAS
DETALLES
HARDTACK HOOKER
JUDY

1936 JOHN CLAY TO VIRGINIA

81

Gastón Santos

it would have to be divided into two chapters. Halfway down the right hand margin appears a name that I discovered with joy: Gastón Santos. He was a handsome young Mexican, son of a great *cacique*, and gifted in two diverse occupations, either one of which would have satisfied most men: he was not only an extremely popular motion picture actor, the Tom Mix of Mexico, but also a first-class *rejoneador*, a *torero* who fought bulls from horseback, often keeping both hands free of the reins in order to place *banderillas* or manipulate the long lance with which he tried to kill the bull from horseback. When this proved impossible, ninety percent of the time, he would dismount, ask for a matador's regular sword and finish the job. He was awesome.

I had known Gastón on prior meetings, had stayed with him at his ranch in central Mexico, and had accompanied him to fights. In later years we had renewed acquaintances when I was serving in Mexico City on a governmental mission. But when I wanted to have him appear in the novel as a *rejoneador*, I had not been able to recall his exact name. Once when I carried no pen or paper for a note, I recovered Santos but not

his first name. Another time I captured a fleeting Gastón but not what followed. Then one day I saw on a village wall a poster giving his full name and, to make sure I remembered it, I took a photograph, then hurried home and jotted down the name here in red ink. Now as I was working on an entirely different problem, I again found his full name.

In Seville John Fulton, Robert Vavra and I had conducted our own sorteo, sorting six bulls into what we thought at the time to be an ideal match to the matadors for my climactic corrida; but as so often happens, when the time came to write the scene the early work proved helpful but not usable, and it required much reworking back and forth, as shown in the illustration on the next page, before I came up with a satisfactory teaming of bulls and matadors. The bold Longford shows that even at this late date I was still trying to find the right name for my lovely young professor, whom I was eventually to discard entirely.

The final of these three illustrations was essential, both for me and for the potential reader. The number of times this page had to be altered proved that even though I had been down this perilous road many times, I still found it difficult to keep a large manuscript under control while trying to remember who was who and when and married to whom. I never have mastered the art and must have at hand a constant reminder. And I suspected that when the New York editors finished reviewing this table they would suggest additional changes.

15. SORTEO

28 July 1991

(handwritten notes, largely illegible)

MRS. EVANS LUNCH.
6 + 1 OUTSIDER / SAN MATEO
MARICON
12 sharp
The cow (REINA)
WORK OUT DETAILS
PLAQUES / JUAN SILVETI
IZQUIERDISTA
They see bombard bull (47)
PREPARE FOR CEMENT
DETAILS FINANCES / LEBESMA

BULLRING + MORONES
TIENTA
3 CIALS
DRESS
CALDERO
TORO DOPED/TORO P

CAL ES

JUDY MORONES + CAPE

CEMENT
2 TAKES

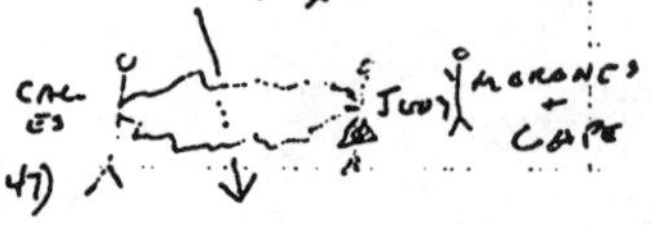

SORTEO 105
DEDICATION 141
SUSTITUTO PEÑUELAS
ACTUAL 229.

#43   25
#4 SANGRE AZUL
44-43   30

30 fog. DEATH SANGRE AZUL

LONGFORD

RANCH 122
BULLS 224
STATS

GUSTAVO MORÓNES
Calero
ALFONSO RAMOZ

SANGRE AZUL
SORTEO
LIZ LANDON
BETSY KING

#	kilos	pounds	age	notes
29	448 kilos	985 pounds	4 yrs 3 months	Veneno wants, sluggish
32	450 kilos	900 pounds		skittish, Veneno does not want
33	433 kilos	955 pounds		placid, maye explosive, Veneno doubtful
38	463 kilos	1o20 pounds		big, sluggish ox, Veneno wants
42	444 kilos	970 poinds		small horns, quick mover, Veneon o wants
47	572 kilos	1040 pounds		not shaved, eager to attack Veneno terrified

Gómez wants	Veneno wants	Sorteo Yields		
		Gómez		VICTORIANO
32	33	Big 38	47	Big unshaved
33	42	Quick 42	33	Placid????
47	38	Over age 29	32	Skittish

1160
2320

Indians	Falafoxes	Clays
500 Drunken Builders		
680 Ixmiq ardent builder Pyramid built		
900 Nopilitzin and pulque		
1051 Altomecs take Toledo		
1470 Tezozomoc leader		
1477 Lady Grey Eyes		
1488 The Hideous Goddess	1498 Antonio Palafox born	
1503 Xuchitl born	1504 Alicia de Guadalquivir	
1521 Stranger born	1524 Palafoxes to Mexico	
1529 Stranger baptized	1531 Cathedral at Toledo built	
1540 Stranger marries Anton	1540 Antonio marries Stranger	
	1548 Veta Madre at Mineral	
	1570 Hall of Government built	
	1575 House of Tiles built	
4 Altomec girls marry Pontifex bishops 2,3,4, 5 and have 23 children	1642 Palafox bushops 2,3,4,5 marry Altomec girls	
	1726 Aqueduct built	
	1740 Mineral at 700 feet	
	1744 1,200,00a A, 2146 Indians	
	1760 Facade of the Cathedral	1823 Jubal Clay born
	1810 Candido Palafox born	1846 Jubal at war in Mexico
	1830 Bulls from Guadalquivir	1847 Jubal visits Mineral Toledo
	1847 Clay sees China Poblano	1864 Jubal at Cold Harbor
	1858 Reform. 450,000 acres	1865 Clay Plantation burned
	1867 Maximilian executed	1866 Clay in exile at Toledo
	1886 Graziela Palafox born	1874 Clay marries Caridad Altomec
1874 Caridad maaries Clay	1897 Eduardo Palafox born	1882 John Clay born in Toledo
	1906 Graziela marries Jhn Clay	1906 John marries Graziela Palaf
	1910 Revolution. 212,000 acres	1909 Norman Clay born Toledo
	1912 Gral Freg stroms Toledo	1917 John Clay with AEF France
	1919 Gral Freg assassinated	1920 Pyramid and Cathedral
	1933 Palafox girl marries N.C.	1933 Nrman C. marries Palafox gi
	1937 Agrarian reform400,000 Ac	1936 John & Norman exile in Aalat
	1938 Expropriation oil wells	1943 Norman C duty in Pacific
	1939 Fausto Palafox killed	1951 Borman duty in Korea
		1959 N.C. visits Hardtack Hooker
1961 Flaco Flores Ixmiq-61	1961 Don Eduardo at Ixmiq-61	1961 Nrman C. at Ixmiq-61

Despite writing problems still to be faced, the gossamer filament, ripped apart so brutally thirty years ago, had been miraculously mended; its fragmented parts too wispy even to be seen had been rewoven. I was not only enabled to move forward, I was commanded to do so.

On the day that Mari ended her treatment, scarred as if she had been burnt, I finished the final chapters of my novel and we left steaming Texas and fled happily to Maine, she with a body that had been cured to the extent that cancer can ever be completely cured, and I with a finished novel, if any work of art can ever be said to be finished.

When I had time to look back upon those disappointing days of 1961 I constructed a reasonable hypothesis of what had happened when things fell apart. I had assembled my papers and photographs in chronological order. I had gathered the three notebooks. I had packaged them for the Library of Congress. I had addressed the package. And I had called the forwarding company. That much is irrefutable.

But I suspect that the forwarding agent never came to pick up the package, and because I had assumed that it had been sent, it was allowed to remain in place for some time. (My family moves an immense amount of paper every week: letters, proofs from my publisher, tax inquiries from overseas inspectors, newly transcribed chapters from my secretary; so it is easy for a particular paper or batch of papers to be lost.) In some general cleanup my carefully prepared package was taken from its mailing spot on the sideboard and removed to a corner of our storage room.

But there my supposition breaks down, for Virginia found the family photographs and the manuscript in two different locations. Did someone open the package to retrieve a particular photograph of more than average interest? Whatever the explanation, events happened as I have stated. Seven people tried vigorously through the years to find the manuscript—Bennett

Cerf, Albert Erskine, Helen Strauss, Owen Laster, John Kings, Mari Michener, Virginia Trumbull—not to mention the searchers in the Library of Congress. I never joined the search because I knew everything was safe somewhere in the Library.

Because John Kings needed photographs for the book of memoirs which Random House was doing, and because my cousin Virginia remembered having seen them, the manuscript was miraculously saved. It was finished under difficult circumstances, edited by Random at what the courts call 'all reasonable speed,' and published. The book that had been killed in mid-flight had, like Lazarus, been lifted from the grave and imbued with new life. The parable in the Book of John does not assure us that this long-dead brother of Martha and Mary enjoyed a long life after his resurrection, but I hope he did.

V. THE PERSISTENCE OF MEMORY

T he outstanding fact in this affair might seem to be that a manuscript lost for thirty years had been recovered with all notes intact. The incident is remarkable. But as I reflect on the matter I see that even more impressive was the high percentage of material in those finished and abandoned chapters that later found its way, almost unwittingly, into later books, some of them only tangentially related to Mexico. It was as if a worthy idea, once generated, could not die but lingered in my mind waiting to be reborn.

Several of my subsequent novels did have obvious relationships with Mexico. In the early chapters of my novel *Caribbean* (1989) I utilized my research on pre-Columbian archaeology, art and religion. I used the great site of Palenque, which became more significant historically with each decade after 1950, but I also utilized the other Mayan civilizations I had studied in 1960. The ideas and understanding I had developed back then remained as clear as if I had deduced them a month earlier. Palenque had exerted a profound impression, and I commend it to all who would like to savor the early days of Mexico.

The force of that powerful site is understandable, but it was my three visits to Tula that produced the strongest single memory of ancient Mexico. Once I saw that cruel but fascinating statue of the reclining *Chac Mool* with his granite stomach-bowl for catching still-warm human hearts, I became a prisoner of his hypnotic power. His image stayed with me always, so it was not surprising that he should force his evil way into the first chapters of *Caribbean*. I could not have kept him out.

It was also obvious that most of what I learned about Spanish culture, as opposed to Mexican, would be used in *Iberia* (1968), my travel reflections on Spain, and specifically my discovery that homeland Spain derived more negative effects than she did benefits from her discovery of gold and silver in the New World. In *Caribbean* I would return to this theme when dealing with the mines in Peru and with the impact of easy money on Spain itself. The penalties were three-fold: first, because Spanish kings had surplus wealth, they were tempted to initiate and prolong adventures in the Netherlands, where the treasure from Mexico and Peru was wasted without ever having helped Spain itself; second, the influx of huge amounts of currency hoisted the prices of goods in Spain, impoverishing the lower classes; third, with this apparent wealth the upper classes could purchase from abroad whatever they desired, causing an appalling abandonment of homeland manufactures. Easily gained wealth is no wealth; real wealth comes from the productivity of the entire nation so that each man can earn something and pay back something in return. It is this lively movement of capital that makes a nation strong, not the accidental arrival of a shipload of silver from a mine in Guanajuato—or from my imaginary mining town of Toledo in central Mexico.

I learned the basic character of Spain from protracted travel in that country; I learned how she abused those characteristics in the New World by studying her governors-general in Mexico.

Because Mexico abuts Texas, when I came to write a long novel about that gargantuan state I was thrown south of the Rio Grande, and all that I knew about Mexico came welling back. I understood Santa Anna; I knew each adventure of the rebel *generalísimos* as they rampaged back and forth across Mexico; I knew about expropriation of oil wells and crazy military invasions of Mexican troops into what would become the United States. The first chapters of my novel *Texas* (1985) focused almost exclusively on Spanish and Mexican themes, which is appropriate since the early chapters of Texas history—forget novels and romances—are exclusively Hispanic themes. It is not until the Civil War that Texas breaks free of its emotional relationships with Mexico, only to see delicate and often irritating contact reestablished during the Díaz era after 1876. The subsequent disruption of relations in the 1930s has never been fully healed, and a major problem of immigration infiltration has erupted in the 1960-90 period. To understand Texas I had to pay attention to Mexico.

Two smaller books also depended upon the work I had done on Mexico and abandoned. In *The Eagle and The Raven* (1990) I drew upon my acquired knowledge of General-President Antonio López de Santa Anna, the eagle of the story and the self-proclaimed 'Napoleon of the West.' I was glad to renew acquaintance with this flamboyant firebrand, eleven different times president of the country, three times exiled for life, twice recalled to lead the nation as its president, three times the military invader of either Texas or the United States. I first fell under his spell, which he exerts on Mexicans and Americans alike, when I read about how he had lost his left leg in a heroic adventure and later had it buried in Mexico City with full military and clerical pomp. He claimed that since his leg had been a principal hero in maintaining the independence of Mexico, it warranted a hero's burial with the salutes of many guns. Santa Anna is the kind of errant comet that flames across the night sky and is remembered.

Several rather minor incidents growing out of the 1961 manuscript also reveal the autonomic workings of a writer's mind. They show how deeply concepts and even individual words persist in memory, as if they had mysteriously achieved lives of their own which would resurrect on their own accord if need arose.

Let me cite the surprising persistence of a name. As far back as 1959, when I first started daydreaming about the possibility of a Mexican novel, I was looking in an old book and came upon the family name Ledesma. After several false starts I remembered it as ideal for one of my principal Mexican characters, the rotund, acidulous and flamboyant bullfight critic León Ledesma. In an almost inspired passage, much longer than what appeared in the published book, I wrote of his intellectual response to bullfighting, but also of his regard for the culture of Spain and its oft expressed fascination with death. I worked and reworked this long account till it approached what I wanted to convey about these two difficult subjects, then laid aside the pages for thirty years.

Decades later, when I was deeply immersed in writing about Spain's dominance of the Caribbean and required a resonant name for my hero, a courageous Spanish admiral who dueled with Sir Francis Drake of England across the Caribbean, I experimented with a handful of usable names, but none seemed appropriate. Then, late one day, the word Ledesma returned to me. As soon as I pronounced it I knew this was it and never reconsidered.

Now there is no way I could have consciously said: 'Jim, years ago in your Mexican thing you had a great name, Ledesma.' I had laid aside that name long ago and had never, so far as I know, recalled it even casually, let alone intentionally. It had vanished from my mind, but obviously not from my subconscious. There, deep down, it had clung to life, so that when I needed it again it surfaced, finding new and vivid adventures.

Even though I neither read nor brood about books I've written long ago, it is still hard to explain how I had typed that name Ledesma so many times in 1961 and then, unremembering, used it happily again thirty years later in another book which required an equal number of typings. I cannot explain this lapse except to say that the name had acquired a will of its own, able to resurface afresh when signals from my searching brain alerted it to the fact that I once again needed it.

So in 1960 when wrestling with my Mexican novel, it was inevitable that I would return to a subject I'd attempted before, and as we have seen, bullfighting with durable Gómez as hero, became a major thread in that work. But it was fated not to be finished, at least not at that time, so Gómez returned to my subconscious. Later, when television sought a comic name for one of its burlesqued characters in the popular series *The Addams Family* based on the horrible-lovable monsters of the cartoonist's fancy, they chose Gómez and, as you might guess, he became a hero. This surprising development erased my bullfighter from my mind. My gallant *torero* Juan Gómez was superseded by the comedian of that name and was lost to me.

Until 1989 Juan Gómez no longer existed, but later that year a gifted secretary who had worked with me in Florida and who knew a good deal about books suggested that she be allowed to gather from my published work the writings I'd done on nature, geology, wildlife and the animal kingdom in general. 'It could,' she argued, 'make an interesting anthology.' I agreed, but when she had assembled the material I said: 'I have two additional stories I've always wanted to write. We'll add them as fresh contributions,' and it was agreed that I'd try to get these captivating yarns down on paper. The first dealt with a gung-ho Army colonel who wages battle with a gray squirrel, Genghis Khan, who steals the expensive sunflower seeds the colonel and his wife place in their garden for their birds. It's a protracted fight between human determination and animal cunning, and I wanted to see it in print in short-story form.

The second proposed addition was a more complex matter. It had started as a simple story about an aging breeder of fighting bulls in Spain who places his faith in the Virgin Mary and is aided by her. From this beginning the plot had acquired so many accretions, twists, and complications that to my surprise it had matured, still unwritten, into a subject for a proper novella of more than a hundred pages, too long for the nature anthology. An interesting aspect was that I had given the villain of my story, a cowardly matador from *Triana*, the gypsy quarter of Seville, the name Gómez without remembering that I had already used it for my Mexican matador, a man of unusual bravery and stubborn honor. In Mexico he had been Juan

Gómez, patterned after a fighter I had known there in 1936; in Spain he became Lázaro Gómez, modeled upon a much different type of fighter I had known there in 1932. Gómez had sprung back to life and was still so vital that he practically wrote my novella for me, once again a fraud and a cheat but nevertheless a shameless survivor, for at story's end he is, as always, triumphant. Apparently I had been powerless to dismiss the name Gómez, for deep in my consciousness rested that fruitful union of a name and a profession. The abstract concept of Gómez had crystallized into the essence of bullfighting, regardless of the locale of the story or the type of man using the name.

Then the timing and coincidence became almost incredible in this exploration into the mysteries of memory. My secretary's note on the manuscript shows that on 20 June 1991 I completed work on the novella, but on the next day, 21 June 1991, my cousin Virginia found the lost manuscript of Mexico. On 26 June the manuscript and three booklets of notes reached me, and I discovered that thirty years earlier I had given one of my matador heroes the name Juan Gómez. Unlikely as it seems, I had completely forgotten that I had done so. When I asked my editors: 'In which book shall I keep him?' they advised firmly: ' In *Mexico* he's such a perfect foil to the other matador that he's got to remain there,' and it was agreed.

The problem then became: 'What do we call him in the Seville novella?' and after half a dozen experiments with Hispanic names that had no resonance whatever for me, we decided upon Lázaro López, which has the two accent marks to remind the reader that it is Spanish and not English, and it worked passably well in the story. But I realized what I had lost when it came time to type out my central paragraph and it read almost lamely 'And there was López.'

My acquaintance with John Fulton is another example of the power of memory, this time in connection with a living human being, not a creature of imagination. Fulton (in Spanish Ful-toné), as I came to know him in the next thirty years after

Matador John Fulton

I had recognized him from his photograph, had courage, determination and arrogance to spare. Despite a wilderness of disappointments and to the surprise of all, he finally managed to become a full-fledged matador in both Mexico and Spain. Never a commanding figure in the taurine world, he nevertheless became an honorable fighter willing to face the deadly Miura bulls other *toreros* elected to avoid, because Miura bulls had a long history of killing matadors.

But Fulton had another arrow in his quiver: he was a fine draftsman who could turn out taurine posters, bullfight sketches, and oil paintings of high quality. He also illustrated books, devised the ornamental capes which matadors carried into the ring at the start of each afternoon's performance, and helped design almost anything related to the ring. After years of exploring a dozen different aspects of drawing and painting, he had made himself into an accomplished artist who earned a precarious living by operating a small art gallery near the Seville cathedral where we had first met. I followed his various careers with quiet attention and marveled at his stubborn insistence upon being a matador and an artist, two of the more difficult professions.

When I finished adapting my short story about the Spanish bullfight scene into a novella, I realized it was too long for the nature anthology and too far removed from its mood. I now visualized an entirely different life for it: 'I'll see if I can find a publisher who will do it as a short novella, and to make it more compelling, I'll ask John Fulton to do twenty full-page drawings and twenty vignettes to adorn the story, and make it a real bullfighting book.' That night I airmailed to Seville the following proposal:

Dear Matador:

I have completed the manuscript of an anthology of the nature episodes I've included in my books through the years, but to the stories already in print I've added two new ones: the comic duel between the retired Army colonel and a gray squirrel who ravages the bird feeder his nature-loving wife keeps supplied with sunflower seeds; and a long novella of about 42,000 words depicting a comparable duel between the Virgin Mary and a gypsy fortune teller in *Triana*, the Virgin backing Don Cayetano Mota, a broken-down, seventy-year-old ganadero who prays for at least one good afternoon with his bulls in Málaga, Puerto de Santa María or Seville; the gypsy backing her brother, Lázaro López, a Cacancho-type six foot beanpole and a real Curro Romero.

As I thought about you, it occurred to me that this bullfight episode might be detached from the anthology and printed separately as a small, handsome book, if, and only if, my friend the matador would wish to provide twenty full-page vertical black-and-white illustrations of top-flight art and dramatic content, plus another twenty vignettes of Seville.

To my delight, Fulton responded quickly that he would enjoy doing the forty drawings, would start immediately when he received a copy of the manuscript, and would pray that I would be able to find a publisher. Much sooner than I had expected, the first batch of preliminary drawings arrived, lively affairs that bespoke Seville during spring Holy Week and the ensuing fiesta with carriages in the park and bullfights each afternoon for eight days. We were on our way.

But then the original Mexico manuscript arrived on my desk and I found myself entangled with not one bullfight story but two. It was obvious that between them there were conflicts about priorities, but it required only brief study to see that the Mexico novel must be given precedence in my writing schedule, in Random's editorial attention, and in positioning on the fall publishing schedule. Once decided, none of us deviated from the decision; all concentrated on the exacting tasks of enabling it to happen.

Lázaro López executing the mariposa, a spectacular cape pass in which the matador holds the cape behind his back, then swings it first to one side then the other like the fluttering of a butterfly's wings. Pen and ink drawing by Matador John Fulton.

But in concentrating on the Mexican novel I was not allowed to ignore the Seville novella because Matador Fulton's illustrations continued to arrive, and they brought back wonderful memories of 1961 when I was visiting the bull ranches with Fulton and acquiring my insights into his unique world. I was especially pleased when he finished reading my story and sent me six pages of little queries about details, including several of magnitude: 'Dear Jim: When the picadors enter the arena in the opening parade, you have them brandishing their long oaken staves. This is an error everyone makes. They enter only on horseback, no lances or pics visible.'

Nothing in writing is ever simple, for when I thought I had all details of the two bullfight stories neatly sorted out, Random House called with distressing news: 'Big problem, Jim. You can't use your title for the Seville novella. You've got to think of something else.'

Way back in 1937 I had decided that if I ever wrote the story it would be called *The Man Who Was A Bull*, focusing on the owner of the bull ranch who was befriended by the Virgin. But as I completed the tale in 1991 I began calling it *The Virgin and the Gypsy*, ideal for a story which emphasized the duel between the Virgin befriending her devoted rancher and the

gypsy fortune teller defending her sleazy brother, who needed all the help he could get. I judged this to be an admirable title, fitting precisely the story I was telling.

My editors agreed with me: 'You're right. It's a marvelous title—so good that D.H. Lawrence used it sixty years ago, but he spelled it *Gipsy*.'

'You can't copyright a title, can you?'

'No, but Random happens to be the American publisher of the Lawrence book and we'd look silly offering two books with the same title. How could the sales and shipping people differentiate between them? You've got to think up another title.'

How irritating! I had been reflecting on the persistence of memory in regard to the contents of my unpublished novel but had not remembered that D.H. Lawrence had written a fine short novel with the title I had adopted. At the time I appropriated it I remember writing a postscript to my secretary: '*The Virgin and the Gypsy* sounds as if it would be a fine title.' My judgment was good, my memory faulty, but not my capability to juggle with the elements of disaster. Like my new hero Lázaro López, born Gómez, I had to come up with something, and after repeated experiments with titles that had no resonance whatever, I came upon *Miracle in Seville*, which summarized the novella precisely.

If the intellectual life of a writer is held together by gossamer filaments which are in daily risk of being fragmented, this insecurity is offset by the tenacity of memory when a good idea implodes in the mind. Concepts, patterns of development, twists of plot, emphases, and even isolated phrases of quality take refuge in back corners of the mind, waiting and ready, sometimes imperatively, to spring back to life. A good story, once devised mentally, can survive in usable form for generations. Nearly fifty years ago I laid out a short story about a Nazi medical doctor working in an orphanage on the French-Belgian border in the 1944-45 period of World War II. I've never written it down, but it reverberates in my memory as one of the best ideas I've had, and apparently it will remain there, ready to be called upon if the time ever ripens.

Because the aspiring writer must depend upon experiences and imaginings that persist for decades, it is important for young people who hope to become writers to accumulate a substantial body of knowledge in their early years, starting no later than eleven—images, understandings and insights into the characters of people around them from which they can later draw. It is such data that will enrich their creative lives. Memory is persistent; ideas do germinate if they exist in a rich culture, and vast concepts can suddenly acquire an inner illumination which makes them usable in forms not even vaguely foreseen while one is acquiring and codifying them. Bright young people who work at attaining insights become writers; dullards who never speculate on anything fail.

There remains the perplexing phenomenon of 'writer's block,' so beloved of biographers and movie makers who delight in portraying the agonized writer who can accomplish nothing when facing the typewriter. I am asked about this constantly and always explain: 'The professional writer never has a writer's block. Of course he has dark periods, but he refuses to submit to them. He moves ahead to some easier part of his manuscript.' Then I add: 'I've done that many times, but I warn you. While jumping ahead does break you out of the impasse, when in the orderly development of your manuscript you reach that spot to which you've jumped, you'll find you can't use much of what you've written. The mood of your writing will have changed. Your characters will have been behaving differently. And what you assumed was an easier bit of writing proves to be just as difficult as the part you bypassed. You saved no time by jumping ahead, but you did break free from being marooned at dead center.'

I believe what I tell my listeners, yet here I'm confessing that in *Mexico* I suffered a block for thirty years, 1961-91; in the case of the Leningrad novel I managed a good start in the 1950s but got knocked down by a heart attack; and the novel on contemporary social relationships never really got a fair start and died forever. On my great idea about the Nazi doctor I've made several desultory starts but accomplished nothing, so I've been blocked since 1945 to now in the mid 1990s . . . if I ever do begin to write it. Writer's block? I've suffered colossal ones, but I no longer surrender to the minor ones lasting a few days or weeks which seem to terrify many writers. Those I exorcize by turning to other work, and I recommend this tactic to others.

VI. THE TEXAS GIRLS

hen I ceased work on my Mexican novel in 1961, I added a paragraph at the end of Chapter 10 which would give the reader a clue as to how the story was going to progress in the final chapters still to be written. Norman Clay, the narrator of the novel, is awakened by the arrival of a touring car at the House of Tile with three noisy Texas girls whose presence would give the novel a bright new twist. I stress this paragraph now because it proves that the Texas girls had been planned as major protagonists in the novel since its inception, even though they inexplicably do not appear in my original outline.

> Now, as the Festival of Ixmiq exploded into full vitality in the plaza below, I left my Spanish ancestors and turned to sleep, for I had been twenty-four hours without any and was exhausted, but before I could close my eyes a car squealed into the plaza and a trio of girls' voices began calling in English, "Norman Clay, get up, you bum!" I crawled over the sleeping body of Ricardo Martín and looked out the window.
>
> The Americans had arrived.

When I resumed work in 1991, I was content to know that I would be working with the three lively women from Texas, a robust state in whose history I had done some work. Since these were women I had seen in my classes and whom I admired, I tried to write of them with understanding and affection. I introduced them in this way, and in this chapter I shall print passages from my original portrayal of these charming girls to help the reader follow what I was trying to do:

I was mistaken when I said that I had been accosted by "a trio of girls' voices," for when the three new-comers piled out to pick up their reservations at the House of Tile I saw that they were not girls. One was in her mid-twenties, another probably in her late teens, and the third a young woman I had known briefly and chaotically in Colorado. They were a ravishing trio, worthy of having some Trojan Paris choose among them as "the fairest of all," and I was both delighted and terrified to see them on the loose here in Toledo. I was not sure that the Festival of Ixmiq-61 was big enough to absorb these three.

To begin with, apart from their exceptional winsomeness, they were in appearance, accent and brashness, typical young Texans, all affiliated with Texas United University in Dallas. When introductions were made I learned that the older woman—although "older" is a misnomer for someone so young—was Professor Liz Longford, in the Department of Sociology. It was she who had proposed the expedition south* as part of a research project, and two of her students had jumped at the chance to spend their spring break with her in Mexico rather than at the more banal whing-ding at Florida's Fort Lauderdale.

The first of her students was red-headed Betsy King, nineteen years old I learned later, and a scholarship student from the west Texas town of Lubbock. Short on spending money, she was long on brains, wit and charm. I liked her from the moment we sat together over an early breakfast, and found constant

---

*Here I state that Professor Longford initiated the trip to Mexico, but on pages 128 and 148 I imply that it was the students who did. Editors are supposed to catch this kind of contradiction, and in this case they did.

amusement in her brash Texas accent and her capacity for making jokes at her own expense. She was the kind of bright-eyed lass who sparked a festival, and I was sure she was going to enjoy this excursion.

I would have no great trouble with these two lively characters, although some readers did question whether a professor would behave with the relative abandon that Dr. Liz Longford did, but the complaints were not disqualifying. However, with the third young woman, most important to the novel, I ran into real and repeated trouble, for she had become, in my writing, something of a sexpot, beautiful and freewheeling and likable. I represented her thus:

> The third young woman, leader of the trio, owner of the expensive convertible and principal driver, was one I knew well and certainly did not want to see coming at me while I was on a working assignment. Judy Hooker, aged twenty-one, was the daughter of a Dallas oil tycoon, and rich because of ownerships he had vested in her, and blessed with a honey-haired beauty that seemed unfair when she had so many other advantages. She was of medium height but weighed only slightly over a hundred pounds, each part of her body harmoniously related to the other, so that she could have been a dancer, a mime, or an actress. Instead she was a provocative little hell-raiser and an adorable companion. She had a gamine smile that started as a speculative side glance, grew into an inquisitive look and sometimes exploded unexpectedly in raucous Texas laughter. To this she added a languid manner and a heavy Texas drawl. My earlier encounter with her had left smouldering emotional ashes and I did not want to see them exacerbated back into flame. To put it simply, Judy Hooker was one too many for me, and we both knew it.

I had met her in 1959 when I was on a three-month assignment in Dallas doing a photographic essay on the flamboyant Texas oil millionaires, and although I came to know some half dozen of them more or less intimately, working and flying and talking with them, I concentrated mostly on Hardtack Hooker, the colorful member of the bunch. Born to an impoverished sharecropper family in Arkansas, he had run away from home at fifteen, worked at a quick succession of jobs, and landed a berth on an oil tanker plying out of the port of Galveston. This unlikely experience accounted for his name, for in later years on the oilfields when food was minimal he assured his young companions: "It's a damned sight tastier than hardtack on some Gulf of Mexico tanker."

When an older Texas owner of one of the oil wells that used his tanker took passage on the ship to see how his crude was being handled, the old-timer found in young Hooker the kind of rough-and-ready hand he had been at that age, and such a warm relationship developed that the oil man offered Hooker a job at one of his holdings in east Texas, where he won repeated promotions and the Texan's youngest daughter as his wife. But Hardtack did not rely only on his father-in-law's millions; as a shrewd manipulator he acquired oil leases adjacent to any that his wife's father operated, and then struck out on his own and picked up some very profitable leases in Louisiana and Oklahoma. Before he was thirty-five he was a hard working, profane, risk-taking prototypical Texas oil millionaire and enjoying the experience.

He was a delight to photograph, for even though temperatures in Dallas often reached one hundred degrees in summer, he dressed in the role he was required to play: boots made of some exotic leather at eight thousand dollars a pair, U.S. Army whipcord cowboy trousers in that soft color called military pinks, a shirt of some alpaca-like fabric from South America at eight hundred dollars, a bolo tie featuring a Navajo emerald set on a silver base, its two ends tailing off into ten-dollar gold pieces, a Mexican style jacket close about the hips and never buttoned in front, sometimes a bandana, and a huge felt sombrero of unblemished fawn which he had steam-cleaned and reblocked at least once a month. But he did not allow his clothes to define him, for he was not only an oil man, he was also a typical ranch owner, narrow hips, wide shoulders, a grizzled sun-burned face with deep lines cutting both cheeks, hard-set blue eyes and raven hair which he wore brushed forward over his forehead. In his big high-heeled boots he walked as if they were quite uncomfortable, and this gave him a side-to-side sway, but he had the capacity to embrace anyone with whom he was talking with his eyes, had always completed his deals in that forthright manner, and men said of him: "His word is as good as his bond—if you already have his bond."

Those who knew him best said: "He drives a hard bargain, but when it's reached he never gloats if it blows in rich or crybabies if it proves dry."

He had three children, two very able sons thanks to the demanding way their mother raised them, and this daughter Judy, now on the loose in Toledo.

I said earlier that I was not comfortable having her on the scene when I was working, for during the third month of my stay in Dallas I became aware that this nineteen-year-old untamed beauty was taking more than a passing interest in how I worked, what my relationships were with my bosses in New York, and how I managed two radically different professions. "Which is hardest," she asked, "catching the right picture or writing about it?"

"When I'm crawling around impossible places to get a good shot, I think: 'Writing is a lot easier than this,' but when I'm at my desk and no words come, or when those that do come aren't in the proper order, I think: 'Photography is so much easier, because there you have control over what you're doing.'"

"What you're saying is that neither is easy."

"You catch on."

"Could you teach me to take pictures?"

"The basics are easy. Sure, if you worked at it and didn't horse around."

"You think all I do is horse around?"

"It could be your principal weakness."

"You sure don't know me. When I want to zero in, Baby-0, can I concentrate."

A series of conversations like this convinced me that she did honestly want to learn more about my two jobs, and one day I told her: "If you ever do want to write, you really must know how to type," and that day she enrolled in a concentrated summer course that advertised a bold new way of teaching, and in two weeks she had an expensive top-of-the-line Royal and a beginning mastery of the QWERTY keyboard. But she also had an equally expensive Nikon camera with four different lenses and she was taking satisfactory pictures.

I believe it was her progress in these fields that prompted her to suggest, one day: "We have this cabin in Estes Park, close to the Rocky Mountain National Park in Colorado. Why don't we fly up there and have an advanced seminar on really using a camera? The scenery's wonderful. Four or five days would do it."

"Can your father break away for that long?"

"He wouldn't want to come. He bought the place but rarely uses it."

"Will your mother join us?"

"She hates the Park. Says it's fine for the men, they're out all day, but it's hell on the women. They have to do the work."

"Well, who. . . ."

"Clay! We don't need anyone. We're going to take some wonderful shots of those wonderful mountains. Wait till you see them."

"You mean. . . ."

"Clay, don't ask a lot of questions." And on those nebulous terms we prepared to fly into the heart of the Rockies, but when it became obvious that we really were going, and alone, Hardtack took me aside and said: "Clay, you strike me as a decent sort. We're about the same age and it's ridiculous for you to go flying off with my daughter. I sure as hell can't tell her what to do, but I can tell you this. If you do anything to dishonor her or get her picture on the front page, I'll track you down and kill you." He did not have to repeat.

When it came time for Judy to bid her mother goodbye, Mrs. Hooker said: "See that the doors are locked when you leave," and I got the impression that when Judy had been about thirteen and beginning to take an interest in boys, her mother had week by week surrendered any attempt to govern her headstrong daughter, and now she preferred not to know what her child was up to.

The flight from Dallas to Denver was a summary of western America: the vast flat plains of west Texas and New Mexico, the gradual appearance of low hills along the New Mexico border, and then the wild explosion of the Rocky Mountains as viewed from above. "More than forty peaks over fourteen thousand feet." Judy said with an excitement that could not have been exceeded had she owned them.

At Denver we rented a Pontiac and as we left the agency she said: "Two roads north. A six-lane highway, you can do eighty if the cops don't nab you. Or a twisty, windy road in the mountains, great views and the real Rockies."

"You're the guide. I'm the driver."

"No," she said. "You're the driver only if we take the highway. If we drive into the mountains, I'm the driver. I love those curves and sudden drops."

"You'd prefer the mountains, wouldn't you? Let's hit them."

"I'd have despised you if you took the highway," and within a few minutes we were in the high country, so close is Denver to its mountains. She had accurately described the roads she was following, for we had constant vistas, a wonderful sense of having the great mountains looking down at us as we wove our way, and as she had predicted, some rather sudden drops off to the east, the side on which I was sitting. She was a confident driver and a good one, but I was especially pleased when she stopped now and then at some majestic panorama to get out of the car and photograph some scene I had recognized as ideal for representing the mix of mountain, forest and plain. She had a sharp eye.

I had heard good reports of Estes Park and its famous Stanley Hotel of old days, but I had discounted the tales of its Alpine-Village charm, with high mountains enclosing it and the engineering marvel of the highway that climbed over twelve thousand feet before descending to western-slope ski resorts like Breckenridge and Steamboat Springs. It was a mountain fairyland, and Hardtack Hooker had one of the luxurious cabins a few miles out of town at the eight thousand-foot mark overlooking a valley filled with deer, elk, beaver and a host of birds. Outside each window hung a vial containing a mixture of sugar and water at which groups of hummingbirds feasted, their tiny wings an invisible whirl, their long beaks dipping into the narrow openings of the containers.

So there we were in the heart of the Rockies to spend five days talking about writing and photographing and with me having no idea what to expect. I was shown a bathroom, but no bedroom, and when I laid out my shaving gear I found ahead of me an expensive shaving brush with an engraved monogram, H.C. Not knowing what to do with it, I placed it off to one side, but when I returned later I saw it was missing.

Although I might have wanted to know who H.C. was, I had no chance to ask, because when I went back to the main room, I found that Judy had left a scrawled note: "Gone marketing," and I was left alone to ponder how this trip was going to work out, but I was spared further speculation when an Indian woman came to check the place and replenish the refrigerator. She told me she was Susan and an Arapahoe: "They wanted us to live on a reservation in Wyoming, but father said 'To hell with that,' and we're doing well in a cottage in town. But it's damn cold in winter, snow this deep."

I watched the familiar way in which she set things right in the cabin, and when she came to the beds she said: "I make them both, but . . . ." and her voice trailed off as if she had faced that problem frequently.

"Do Mr. and Mrs. Hooker come here often?"

"Not them. Not the boys, neither, they work too hard. This mostly for Judy, and her friends." She stopped her work and asked: "What do you do? Your name?"

"Norman Clay. I work in New York. That is, New York gives me orders and I go where they send me."

"Doing what?"

"I take photographs then write about them, and they both appear in a magazine. Or maybe a book."

"Would I know the magazine?" Enjoying her friendly, inquisitive manner, and appreciating this opportunity to learn more about the cabin, I told her the name of the magazine, and she cried: "I know that. Sometimes people who stay here leave copies," and she rummaged about to find two back copies of my journal: "Anything by you in here?" When I checked I said: "No, but that's what I do."

"Must be fun," and I said: "I came to Texas to write about Mr. Hooker," and she cried: "He one tough man. They tell me 'You cross Mr. Hooker he cut your bags off.' But he real good to me. That Ford out there, he gave it so I can come up here to tend the cabin."

"But he never comes up?"

"Maybe once a year. Maybe a big hunting party for his friends."

"Surely there's no hunting in the Park?"

"North of here, outside the boundary, all you want."

When she left I still didn't know what the sleeping arrangements were going to be, but now had additional proof that Hardtack Hooker, the owner of the cabin, was a dangerous customer. There was a knock on the door, and it was Susan: "Mr. Clay, word of warnin'. You're eight thousand feet up. Oxygen may be rare. Do not run up hills. Takes maybe three days to adjust. You older man, take it easy. Good luck." When she was finally gone I began to feel that the oxygen really was limited, so I lay back in a comfortable chair, propped my feet up and slept.

It was suppertime when Judy reappeared with an armful of purchases and a noisy exuberance: "Wake up, you sluggard. I've chopped a cord of wood for the fireplace, and you should be bringing some in. It gets quite cold," and as she nudged me from my chair she leaned down and kissed me lightly, the first time this had happened.

Reaching out, I caught her wrist and pulled her down on my lap, where she sat comfortably, stretching her bare legs sideways across mine. "What gives?" I asked with a real kiss, and she said: "I've never known an artist, a writer that is. Sounds like a marvelous job. Social significance and all that."

"How far are you in your education?"

"Junior* at Texas United."

"Doing well?"

"When I'm interested."

"Well, you're too young to be up here with me. I'm almost as old as your father."

"He chases girls as young as me. More power

---

* I append an editorial note regarding the probable age of a character. I wrote about her at various times and varied in my intentions. These matters are rectified in reworking a manuscript. The editor noted: 'Here in 1959 Judy is 19 and a junior. Two years later in Toledo she's 21 but still a student, although she should have been graduated in 1960. Better to make her a sophomore here in 1959, then she's still a senior in 1961. See pp. 105 and 136.'

to him."

"He can get away with it. In Dallas he writes his own rules," and I started to push her away, but she would not leave.

"Clay, don't make a big thing of it. This is no big deal," and that night we used only one bed. When Susan appeared next afternoon, for she had learned not to disturb Judy before midday, she smiled at me and said: "That's nice," and as she worked about the cabin she whistled.

* * *

The next four days were ones of joy and confusion. At fifty I had surrendered any likelihood that I would have intimate relations with any woman, my marriage having gone on the rocks, and if it did happen it could not possibly be with a woman so much younger. The idea that I share the passionate love of a world-class beauty was preposterous. Yet it was happening, and abundantly so. We took photographs, we toured the high passes, we drove north over back roads into Wyoming, and we sat for hours watching deer and hummingbirds. We went to bed at midnight, rose at noon, and each night this exquisite young woman was more delightful than before.

She surprised me by talking freely of her desire to know different types of men before she settled on one, and said some astonishing things: "I know I'm going to be quite wealthy, Pop's taken care of that, and the boys I've gone with have known it, too, so I could never be sure whether they chased me for me or my money." She laughed when she said this, lying in bed. "I'm chuckling, Clay, because I never knew whether they'd be able to abide me if I suddenly found myself without money."

We discussed various aspects of the money-sex

relationship, then she said: "My two brothers, God bless them, went to Texas United before me, so that when I entered two years ago, I had a dozen ready-made introductions to the neatest guys on Fraternity Row. Athletes, bookworms, Christers, they were all available, but I've never known a real brain like you, or an artist, either. So for me you're a two-fer, and I'm enjoying every minute of this because it's about time," and after statements like that we were off to lovemaking again.

I was painfully aware that she deserved someone far younger than I, but when I asked what kind of man she was going to marry when her exploring days were over, she squealed: "Marry? That's way down the line. I'd like to date an astronaut, maybe. Some-one who might fly off into space. Or an African explorer, the Nile and the temples. Or," and I remember where and when she said this: "maybe a Spanish bullfighter. The moment of truth, you know."

It was a tumultuous experience, but also infinitely tender, for I was as thoughtful of her needs as I could be, and she was always aware that this was only an exploration on her part and that she was using me in a cynical sort of way. But I was so overjoyed to be allowed to be with her that such considerations were inconsequential. We were having great fun for five days in the high Rockies and to me at least that was an unexpected gift.

But as the visit to Estes drew toward its close I had to worry about what definitions Hardtack Hooker had in mind when he warned me: "If you do anything to dishonor my daughter, I'll track you down and kill you." In the old days that would have included taking a nineteen-year-old girl into the mountains for an afternoon, but to take her there for five nights meant certain death. I had also been

taught the time-honored tradition, inherited from
Europe and particularly from good families in
England, that for a suitor to seduce a daughter in her
father's house was an act beyond the pale. I believed
that, so I was willing to grant Hardtack at least three
grounds for gunning me down. On the last night,
when we had our final celebration in bed, I asked:
"Any chance your father will hear about this?" and
she cried: "Clay! Susan has telephoned him every day
to assure him that things are all right," and before I
could gasp, she added: "She always does."

Since I had done nothing to get Judy's picture
on the front page, I concluded that my survival was
likely, but when we returned to Dallas I found it
difficult to interview Hardtack any further about
Texas petroleum customs and flew back to New
York.

As soon as the Texas gals, the name they called themselves,
joined us in Toledo they went energetically to work, trying to
make contact with any matador or ordinary *torero* who came
their way. On Saturday morning, the second day of the festival,
they prowled the Terrace off the hotel seeking prey, in the
course of which they talked with Norman Clay:

The most important conversation, for me at least,
was the one I could not escape, with Judy Hooker.
Now, two years after our escapade in the High
Rockies, she was sitting across from me at one of the
Widow Palafox's breakfast tables, more alluring than
ever because of her more mature appearance, deport-
ment and intelligence. By subtle messages she had
let me know that she had no romantic interest in me
whatever. Our five golden days together had happened not two years ago but two hundred, and she
now had other pursuits: "Do you remember, Clay,
that I told you when you were working with my

Terrace at the hotel

father that one of these days I'd like to meet a Mexican matador?"

"You said Spanish."

"You can't drive a convertible to Spain. Besides, Liz and Betsy wanted to come along, and they'd like to meet some bullfighters, too."

"Why?"

"Well," Judy said reflectively, "we came because it's pretty hard to meet one if you stay in Dallas. Besides, Liz felt she had to have a look-see in Mexico to complete her research."

"Is this handsome young woman your professor?"

"She is."

"And you call her by her first name?"

"What else? She isn't fifty." With these words she let me know that this year my age signified a great deal, so I said: "I prefer the German pattern. It's Herr Doktor Professor Heimratt, with a slight bow of the head, and don't you forget it."

"So when I read in the gossip column that my old friend Norman Clay was attending the Festival in his home town of Toledo, I told the girls. . . ."

"Now the professor is a girl?"

"Till the age of thirty. I told them: 'I'm sure my old pal will fix us up with some matadors,' and here we are."

"Matadors I do not know intimately, but my uncle is owner of one of the biggest bull ranches in Mexico, and I can certainly fix up a deal for you to go out there for a fiesta tomorrow. . . ."

"Tomorrow is too late. We saw the fights yesterday, and in the stands I saw this real hunk, and when I asked who he was, they said 'Fermín Sotelo, he's fighting tomorrow.' I'd love to meet him. Tried to yesterday, but then the other man got killed and things fell apart."

Now red-haired Betsy spoke: "That death was pretty awful. Does that happen pretty often?"

"First one I ever saw. Photographed it every inch of the way. It'll be a sensation in New York."

"Is that all you thought about?" she asked.

"That's my job, to think about exactly such things, with a camera."

"He also writes," Judy broke in. "He did a fantastic look-read job on my father. Pops said: 'The photos are a lot better than the words.' I thought the opposite."

I was about to ask Professor Longford what she could be researching in a city like Toledo, for I was attracted to her trim appearance, her neatly bobbed hair and flashing eyes—plus the fact that she was much older in all ways than her two girls—when Judy uttered a loud gasp and whispered: "My God! It's fate. There he is," and when I looked across to one of the two larger tables reserved during the Festival for matadors and their troupes, I saw that it was indeed Fermín Sotelo, a lithe, handsome young man of twenty-odd who had recently taken his doctorate, as bullfight circles called the act of progressing from apprentice to full-scale matador. He'd done well in Mexico and so-so during his first expedition to Spain, and the local impresario had probably picked him up for a reasonable fee to fill the third spot on today's card. His exaggerated swagger, the cocky angle of his dark head, the effusive attention paid to him by his subalterns, all testified to a matador on his way up, and I understood why Judy Hooker was so excited about the possibility of meeting him.

"Could you possibly take me over?" she begged,

and I felt ashamed at having to say: "I really can't. I don't know him," and I feared she might think I had declined because I was jealous about her interest in him and not me. That was not the case. I had dismissed our ecstatic five days as a fortunate accident which bore no relationship to the present. She was as desirable as ever, but she had been promoted far above my reach.

But then León Ledesma appeared in his black cape and I flagged him down: "Don León, pull up a chair," and I introduced him to the Texans, to whom he reacted as if they were young royalty: "I adore young women from the state that was cruelly stolen from us by the ancestor of this infamous Norman Clay. Are you all in oil?" When I told him that Liz Longford was a university professor he said: "I would have thought at her youthful age, kindergarten," and she nodded with a captivating smile.

"The problem," I explained, "is that these fine young women are desperately eager to meet a real matador and right over there is Fermín Sotelo having his breakfast. Could you possibly take this young lady, who speaks acceptable Spanish, over to his table and tell the matador that she's your niece?"

"I'll do better. I'll tell him she's my adopted daughter and that if he isn't nice to her I'll give him a scathing review."

Enjoying the charade, Ledesma took Judy by the hand and led her to where Fermín sat with his men. They rose, Ledesma spoke, and Judy fulfilled her ambition. She was talking with a certified *matador de toros* whom she could soon see performing in the ring. As I looked at the pair, each perfect in his or her chosen field, I suffered real envy and felt every day of fifty-two.

Back at our table, Ledesma was a delightful treat for the remaining two Texans, flirting with the professor and treating red-headed Betsy as his eight-year-old niece: "Now what would you do with a matador if I did find you one?"

"She didn't need lessons," Betsy said, indicating Judy who was charming the *toreros* at the big table.

"True, but she has certain assets which make conversation easy," and Betsy snapped: "Are you suggesting I haven't?" Ledesma replied: "Any more insolence from you, Bobbysoxer, and I'll take you over my knee."

He then turned to Professor Longford and asked: "Must I find you a matador, too?" and she said: "I came to listen to the music, not to dance."

Turning to me he asked: "Why is it, Clay, that every year at Ixmiq we get this flood of beautiful American college girls who come down here to find excitement at our Festival? Have they no entertainments at home? No attractive young men? No romance?"

Dr. Longford answered for me: "You saved the right word till last, Señor Ledesma. Romance. You damned Mexicans have very cleverly constructed a myth about Mexico as the home of adventure, starlit nights and guitars." She broke into song: "South of the Border, down Mexico way," and he joined, in Spanish.

In the congenial ambience of a Mexican festival there is much casual conversation among people who have only just met, and some of it, as visitors wait for the next fight to begin, is pleasantly revealing, not only of personal character but also of the general mood:

It was now half after three, but still the Terrace was filled with people who would be attending the afternoon fight. They talked, had a few drinks, compared

notes about the forthcoming fights, and savored the
narcotic ambience of the public plaza. At our table
the conversation took a most unexpected turn when
Professor Longford casually spoke of her two students who had been so determined to find themselves
some matadors, and Mrs. Evans said: "At their ages
I was mad for John Barrymore, and it did me no
harm," and Dr. Liz said: "But you probably had a
normal crush about which you did nothing. When
Judy Hooker develops a crush she will knock down
buildings."

"Did you say Hooker? Of Dallas?"

"Yes. That's her family."

"American Petroleum?"

"Yes. Her father's supposed to be the volcano
that keeps A-P exploding."

Mrs. Evans clapped hands, laughed joyously,
and told us: "Hardtack Hooker, a cross between a
barracuda and a gila monster. My husband fought
that conniving son-of-a-bitch on every oil field in
three states, but we remained good friends. I knew
Judy when she was three months old. Where is she
now?"

"Upstairs in bed," Dr. Longford said, "with one
of the matadors in today's fight."

"You mean. . . sex right before a big fight?"

"They say it goes with the profession. So many
girls attracted to matadors."

"Paul was incommunicado for six hours after,"
Mrs. Evans said, and Dr. Longford continued:
"Theoretically I'm their chaperone."

"You have two of those tigers to look after?"

"They said before we left Dallas. . . ."

"Are you their college professor?"

"I am. They announced that they were on the prowl for bullfighters and they promised that if they found an extra, I could have him."

"Big-hearted girls. But given the alterations in society since when I was young I'd say that today I'd probably be much like them. But with a college professor in the act, too! I'm sure I must know members of your board of regents, big oil and all that."

"No use reporting me to them," Dr. Longford chuckled. "They're glad to have me as a voice to the younger generation, the ones they can't talk to."

When they asked Ricardo his opinion I did not hear his answer, because I was tormented by the vision of Judy Hooker upstairs with her matador occupying the place I had shared two years ago, but that problem was alleviated when she came blithely onto the Terrace to ask: "So when do we start for the arena?"

"Where's Betsy?" Dr. Longford asked, and Judy explained: "She and her handsome centaur went out to the plaza to see his horses. Like all proper Texas girls, she loves horses."

"She wasn't upstairs?" Mrs. Evans asked, rather improperly I thought, and apparently so did Judy, for she said abruptly: "How should I know? She left a note on our table."

"Don't take it so brusquely, Miss. I used to dandle you on my knee when you were two." This reprimand caused Judy to reach for a chair and ask: "Who are you?"

"My husband, Paul Evans of Tulsa, and your father. . . ."

"You're Elsie Evans?"

"That's a first name I try to forget, but yes, our

families were often a team, more often bitter enemies
. . . during some deal."

"Did you know that this rascal, Norman Clay,
wrote that long article about Hardtack?"

Mrs. Evans gaped, stared at me again and said:
"I read it. Great photos of a true rascal, but your text
missed the real Hooker. He was a mean bastard,
excuse me Miss."

"My words exactly," Judy said, "but he does get
what he wants. And he did build his company."

I was now faced with the obligation of setting in motion the
two love stories on which I had planned to concentrate. Somehow or other Judy Hooker must meet up with Victoriano Leal,
the master matador, and for contrast sparkling little Betsy King
must find the rather pathetic peon, Flaco Flores, lowliest member of the Gómez troupe:

> This delay gave me time to visit with my friends on
> the Terrace at the House of Tile, where I found the
> Texas girls serving as the focus of attention. At a large
> table midway between the two reserved for the
> matadors of tomorrow's culminating exhibition, Vic-
> toriano Leal and his team on the west, Juan Gómez
> with his men on the east so as to be near the cafe
> where Lucha Gonzales would be singing, the three
> women reigned like young queens. Judy Hooker,
> with no man at her side, Matador Fermín having left
> immediately after his triumphant fight, had ordered
> two huge pitchers of *sangría* and a half a dozen glasses
> with which she was offering drinks to anyone who
> stopped by her table. When she saw me she cried:
> "Thank God! a man," and to her companions she
> said: "He's not much but he does wear pants," and
> catching my arm, she pulled me down beside her.
>
> Lively as ever and as outspoken, she said: "Señor

Clay, you brought me good luck. I told you I was determined to meet a matador, and you arranged it. Fermín and I had a night I'll never forget."

"Have you lost him?"

"He had to move on to a fight in Monterrey tomorrow. Asked me to go with him, but I couldn't leave these two alone," and with real affection she reached out to grasp the hands of her companions. This action left her face-to-face with Betsy King, and Judy said: "Señor Clay, we must do something about this poor girl. She's come all this way to meet a bullfighter and so far she hasn't even spoken to one."

"They're not on beck and call, you know, Miss Betsy," I said and she replied with that raffish redhead wit that I had appreciated yesterday: "I'm going to meet a bullfighter if I have to go to the fight tomorrow naked," and I assured her: "If you do that, you'll meet a lot more than bullfighters."

Turning serious, she said: "I'd like at least to speak with one of them. Otherwise I've taken four years of Spanish in vain."

"Where did you do that?"

"San Antonio.* Down there you have to learn Spanish or you miss half the fun, the good half."

"You have that in your favor. I've photographed a lot of these *toreros*. . . ."

"Is that the same as matador?"

"It covers the entire ring. The matadors, the men who run the bulls with capes dragging, the men with the sticks, the men on horseback."

"But the man who gets killed sometimes, he's

* I never got around to reconciling Betsy's four years of Spanish in San Antonio with the fact that she's a native of Lubbock and now a nineteen-year-old student in Dallas.

the matador?"

"Wrong. Once you step in that ring with a Spanish bull anyone can get it, and they do."

"But yesterday it was the matador?"

"Indeed." And she said: "All right. A *torero* will do. When I get back on campus I've got to be able to say 'Yes, I dated a bullfighter,'" and Judy, who heard this, said brightly, "Time's wastin', Kiddo. Better get with it."

Seeing a young man she had met leaving the fight, she grabbed Betsy and dragged her to talk with the prospect, leaving me alone with Professor Longford, who seemed concerned with the problem that faced the other girls: How to meet a man? "Who was that attractive American boy? They said he was sleeping in your room?"

"Interesting fellow, Richard Martin from San Diego. Down here he goes under the name of Ricardo Martín," and I pronounced it the Spanish way Mar-TEEN.

"Why the Spanish bit?"

"Fancies himself a matador . . . some day . . . in the ring at Tijuana."

"I thought it was Tiajuana, four syllables."

"So does everyone else. I believe the dictionary even gives that as the preferred pronunciation, Tee-uh-HWAN-uh. But to us Mexicans it's Tee-HWAN-uh."

"I'd like to meet Matador Martín."

"Don't tell me you're scouting for a bullfighter, too."

"At my age and his? No thanks. But I very well might like to write about him."

"In what way? You seem to know little about the bulls."

"But I know a great deal about the effect of bullfighters on young Texas girls. We have Nuevo Laredo on our doorstep, you know. Our college girls run down there now and then."

I drew back: "Sounds like you're writing a romance about the Texas millionheiress Judy and the Monterrey toreador Jesús?" and I sang a few bars from *Carmen*.

"No," she laughed, her pretty bobbed hair glistening in the light from the torches that now surrounded the Terrace. And she responded with her own selection from *Carmen*, the fortune-telling scene. "I'm doing a study of the new American patterns of courtship. The infamous Spring Break in Fort Lauderdale. The skiing trips to Sun Valley. The cruise-ship bit, believe me it's catching on. The car pool. The work place." She paused, studied me for a moment and said: "It's a whole new ball game, as I believe you learned when you did your profile on Hardtack Hooker."

"So you discussed me on the way down?"

"No. I listened on the way down when they discussed you. Don't blush. She gave you high marks . . . for a guy your age."

"I was younger then." Now it was my turn to study her, that face so handsomely modeled, and without a blemish, the high forehead, the dark eyes, and the bobbed hair she manipulated so enticingly. She was a captivating young woman, this lecturer from Texas United, and I wished I were thirty again. "Where did you do your studies?" I asked and she replied: "Brandeis," and I asked: "Jewish?" and she said: "Inexpensive, since I could live at home."

"Don't tell me, but you're going to use Judy Hooker as your archetypal amoral young rich girl?"

"Oh, I'm not a snoop. I'm using her as the

liberated adventuress. Did you ever hear of Isabella Bird, did my master's thesis on her. An English woman, went everywhere, did everything."

"When?"

"Turn of the century. This century."

"Sexual bit, too?"

"Sex wasn't such a big thing then. Or maybe better to say freedom in sex wasn't allowed to women then."

When Judy returned to our table, Professor Longford said: "When this young lady invited me to come along, knowing I was dying to do so, she promised me she'd land a matador. To help me with my story. And she did, so the trip's a success."

"Let's make it two," Judy said brightly, her eyes flashing, and when I turned to see what had activated such interest I saw that Veneno Leal and his three young men had come onto the Terrace and were standing imperially and obviously disturbed to find their table occupied by American tourists. Madame Palafox, anxious to avoid a scandal on the eve of the featured fight, hurried up and told the visitors that their table had been reserved for tomorrow's star matador. I expected a rumpus, but the four tourists, Americans, graciously rose, bowed and said in passable Spanish: "Matador, it's a pleasure, and tomorrow good luck," but they had identified the wrong young man as the matador, choosing the least important of the men, Diego, the good looking *peón* . . . not even a *banderillero*.

The Leal men, appreciating the humor of the mistake, began to laugh, whereupon Veneno said with Spanish charm: "You picked the wrong one. This is the matador, Victoriano. This one," and he gave his younger son a slight cuff on the shoulder, "he's a nobody. He sweeps up after the mules." At

Veneno punishing his son's bull

this exchange of pleasantries, everyone within hearing joined the laughter, and an incident which might have been embarrassing passed, with Veneno asking Señora Palafox to serve the tourists at their new table a bottle of good wine.

"Who are those enchanting men?" Judy asked, and I pointed to the big poster adorning the wall of the cafe next door, where Lucha would be singing. In bright, bold letters it contained the two names "VICTORIANO-GÓMEZ MANO A MANO" which meant that they would each fight three bulls, hand-to-hand, no other full matador in the ring.

At that moment Victoriano had just taken his chair and was adjusting himself in it so as to present his best profile to his fans, and he was a most handsome object, not an ounce of fat, black hair long and tied with a black ribbon in the matador's *coleta* at the nape of his neck, and grave of countenance. "My God, isn't he gorgeous?" Judy whispered, and she tugged on my arm to encourage me to introduce her. I had photographed Veneno and his team several times at other festivals but I could not claim to know them well, but Judy was so insistent that I shrugged my shoulders, took her by the hand and moved the few steps to Veneno's table: "Señores, I'm the photographer who came here to write about you. We've met in Mexico City and Tijuana. This is an *aficionada* from Texas, Señorita Judy Hooker. Her father used to work in your oilfields at Tampico."

The men rose and Victoriano pulled a chair from another table, seating Judy beside him, and the evening was off to a galloping start, but before I had time to return to my table and resume my conversation with Professor Longford, there was another burst of excitement as Matador Juan Gómez came out of the crowd in the plaza, climbed the few steps to the Terrace, bowed stiffly to the Leals, turned to the right and sat his men down at the table next to the cafe where Lucha was preparing to sing. But they were scarcely seated when a nondescript *peón* whom Gómez had picked up cheap for this fight, a man of all tricks in the arena, saw me and remembered that I had once made a fine shot of him placing the *banderillas* and came to greet me. Gómez, seeing his man come to my table, rose slightly and bowed, aware that he also needed all the good photographs of his work possible.

The *peón*, a man from Guadalajara who fought under the name Flaco Flores, "Skinny" Flores because of his meager frame, now sat at our table, and I told the professor and Betsy King, who had rejoined us, what a valuable assistant to the matador he was, making both his position and his performance in it somewhat more important than it was. But once it

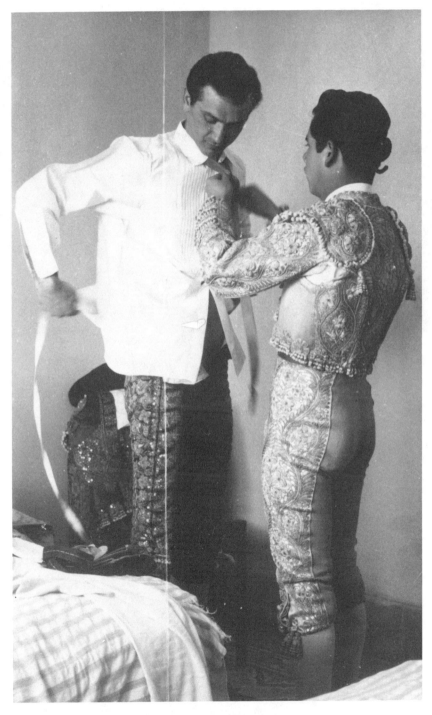

Dressing the matador

Pastoral scene at a bull ranch

was established that he was a verifiable bullfighter Betsy, with her rather good Spanish, told him how interested she was in bulls. After some minutes of taurine conversation Flaco left us to ask Gómez if he might take Betsy to their table, and the matador nodded.

One of the most highly regarded of the festivities of the taurine world is the excursion into the countryside to visit one of the great bull ranches during a *tienta,* a day when the young cows are being tested for their bravery. As I've stated before, it has been well established through the centuries that the inherent bravery of a Spanish fighting bull, and the precise quality of that bravery, depends not on the majestic and powerful bull who was its father, but specifically on the character of the cow who was its mother.

At my *tienta* at the Palafox ranch, the two youngest Texas

Fighting bulls at their ease in the campo

girls will take part and young Betsy will meet not some lowly *peón* but a striking aspirant about to become a full-fledged matador:

> I explained to the Texas girls sitting near me that the cow really had no horns, that is, none that had reached a stage of development where they pointed forward: "So getting hit by the cow is much like getting struck by a flat object. It pushes you about but it doesn't puncture."
>
> As I said this, the third cow was allowed in and when Calesero saw in the first pass that she charged straight and hard and true, he motioned to his partner Morones to take the cow to a far part of the ring and then he astounded me by coming to where I sat and inviting not me but Judy Hooker to come down with him and try her luck. Had the invitation

been for me I would have demurred, but not Judy. With a bound from her seat and a lovely vault over the low fence, she joined Calesero who handed her one end of his cape while he held firmly to the other. He then signaled to Morones to bring the cow over, and when the fiery little animal, aching for a fight, looked up she saw an inviting target, a man at one end of a yellow cape, a tag girl at the other, and between them a stretch of fluttering cloth. In the moment before her charge I thought: "What an appropriate symbol for the festival! A matador whose life task has been to present a handsome figure, a beautiful young woman who insists upon the costume perfect for the moment, the band of color and beyond, that ferocious little bundle of black energy preparing to wreck the place. With my automatic camera I shot six exposures, and in the last one caught Matador Morones in his own fine costume whispering to Judy: "Feet firm. Don't move. Hold the cape tight."

As I clicked off my last shot I gasped, for in my viewfinder the young woman was perfection, and I thought: "Did I spend five days in Estes Park with that gorgeous thing . . . wondering whether I was going to be shot when the affair ended?"

I had no time for an answer, for the cow made a ferocious lunge forward, passing right between the two humans. Now came the critical part, for Morones yelled at Judy: "Turn with him! Plant your feet! Hold tight!" and again the cow smashed right into the middle of the cape, but this time she turned with such incredible swiftness that Judy had no time to prepare. The cow was upon her, butting her sharply in the right leg and tossing her in the air, but she did not fall back onto the sand, for Morones caught her, held her in the air, and delighted the crowd by kissing her on the cheek as he stood her

Calesero parading with ears and tail

back up.

"Toro!" warned the crowd, for the cow, seeing this new center of action, was bearing down on the pair, but Calesero adeptly interposed himself in front of Judy and led the cow away.

I supposed that this was the end of Lady Judy's performance, but I was mistaken. Jarred by the cow's attack and ashamed of having allowed herself to be knocked down, she recovered her end of the cape, handed the other end to Morones and indicated that she at least was ready for another charge. Now it was

Calesero who stood at her side, coaching: "Feet firm.
Hold tight," and it was either her skill or Morones',
but the cape had been placed perfectly, for the cow
roared safely past, but again, even before Calesero
could reposition Judy, the little beast was upon her
from the rear. This time Judy went up in the air, not
down on the ground, and this gave Morones a chance
to catch her before she crashed.* As he planted her
gingerly back on the ground, he again kissed her,
then held her hand aloft as he coached her in taking
a turn of the arena to wild applause from the
watchers. She had scored a triumph as a Texas
cowgirl in neighboring Mexico. And that is the way
Judy Hooker of Dallas, a junior at Texas United
University, met her third full *matador de toros* in three
days. He sat with her during the fourth cow, and a
young aspirant assisted Calesero, who satisfied himself that this cow, too, ran true. Thereupon he came
back to where I sat and invited Betsy King to become
his partner, and she almost leaped into his arms, so
eager was she to give it a try. As she left me she cried:
"Get a picture of this," and within moments she was
holding her end of the cape and responding to
Calesero's coaching in English: "This one not charg-
ing. We go forward, stamp the foot," and this girl of
nineteen who had never even ridden a horse, moved
steadily forward with the matador, stamping her foot
in time with his and shouting like him "Eh! Toro!"
And when the cow finally charged, coming closer to
Betsy than to the matador, she stood firm, and cried
as the cow swept past: "Hey, toro!"

I caught three fine shots of her, one her first
fine pass, one whirling with Calesero to meet the next

---

*I apparently became so enamored of the idea of Morones' catching
Judy in the air that I inadvertently had him do it twice.

charge, and one with the young man who had replaced Morones, embracing her as a champion. And that was how Betsy King of the same university in Dallas met her *torero*, not a full matador yet but in the opinion of many destined to be one some day soon.

During the final fight on Sunday afternoon, the various strands of the novel reach a climax, the most unusual being a miraculous performance by Flaco Flores, the otherwise pathetic *peón* whom Betsy King had picked up. The superlative act is dedicated to her:

> For Gómez the afternoon was degenerating into a debacle. The only splendid moment of the fight did not, unfortunately involve him. True to his promise to Flaco Flores, the *banderillero* he had picked up on the cheap from Guadalajara, he allowed the skinny fellow to place the second pair of sticks, having himself messed up the first pair. The eager substitute must have been rehearsing what he would do this day, if he got a chance to show the skills he knew he had but which others did not recognize, ever since he met Betsy King last night. Now he took the sticks, decorated with garish purple tissue paper wrapped about their length, strode manfully to where Betsy sat above him in the front row, and with the sticks in his left hand he pointed the barbed ends at her and announced he was dedicating his performance to her. The crowd cheered and Betsy, sitting with his frayed entrance cape still gracing the railing, started shouting in a most unlady-like voice: "Mr. Clay! Mr. Clay! Get the photo!" I did, and caught one of the heavenly moments of a bullfight.
>
> Heart pounding, nerves alert, wearing the one decent suit of lights he owned, Flaco went out toward the middle of the arena and started that long, dream-

like stalk toward the bull, jumping up and down now and then to hold the bull's attention. Fortunately, considering what the *peón* had planned, the bull initially remained cautiously immobile, watching the thin figure approach with his arms extended over his head, until finally, with a mad rush, he came out of his defensive position driving right at the man. At that moment Flaco ran toward the bull, made a complete three-hundred-and-sixty degree turn to the left, and wound up facing the now-bewildered bull only a few feet away. Up in the air leaped the man, sticks still high above his head, and with a deft turn and twist of his body he escaped the horns but left himself high enough in the air to enable him to place the barbed sticks exactly in the neck muscle behind the horns.

My automatic camera had caught some dozen shots of those last electric moments. One which showed the full drama and grace of that last turn and downward dip of the sticks would be widely circulated in Mexico as The Pair of Toledo. In a poster-size reproduction paid for by Judy Hooper* it would come to rest on the wall of Betsy King's dormitory room at Texas United in Dallas, beside it a small shot of Flaco dedicating the famous pair to her. It had happened. She had gone to Mexico to meet a bullfighter and she had found a champion.

In the bittersweet aftermath of the final fight, I knew that the adventures of the three Texas girls had to find reasonable

---

* Observe that on this page and the next I use the name Judy Hooper, my original spelling, and exactly right for her. But when dealing with her father the name Hardtack Hooker also precisely denoted him. He won, to the detriment of his daughter who was left with the pejorative Hooker, one of the reasons, perhaps, that my editors did not like her.

conclusions, and I labored long to find them:

> The last fight had been such an emotional affair that there had to be a letdown, and as participants in the Festival gathered in desultory manner at the various tables on the Terrace, one could detect a certain vacancy in their eyes, as if the fires of the last three nights had left only smoldering embers.
>
> The Texas girls were especially deflated. Judy Hooper had seen her current hero, Victoriano Leal, carted off to the hospital with a wound that would force him to miss several fights and the rich contracts they represented. Betsy King was preparing to abandon her gangling *banderillero* Flaco Flores of the Gómez troupe in favor of Gustavo Morones, the dazzling young matador she had met at Don Eduardo's little fiesta, but since it now looked as if her new choice had stood her up, she was furious. And Professor Longford needed several more hours of interrogation with Ricardo Martín, but he was in jail. They were a disconsolate trio, a most unlikely sight at a festival, three young women of above average appearance sitting without any men in the popular gathering spot. It would be interesting to see what pairings developed as the night progressed, but that something would happen I could not doubt, for these Texas gals, as they often called themselves, were on the prowl.
>
> But I was not prepared for the form this prowling was to take, for when I returned to the Terrace I found a distraught Judy Hooper eager to enlist my assistance in a project which absorbed her: "Clay, I've got to see Victoriano. He needs me."
>
> "He's safely in the hospital. Reports are hopeful. And he doesn't need you, he needs sleep."
>
> "I went there, but they wouldn't let me in."

"I should think not. You're no relative."

"I'm more. And I'm sure he's worrying about me."

"Judy! If he's bothering to worry at all, it's about his contracts."

"If you won't call Don Eduardo, I will."

"Why him?"

"Because in Toledo he's in charge. So, please, call him."

Under such pressure, repeated with tears, I did telephone Don Eduardo, and reluctantly he came to the hotel, picked up both Judy and me and drove us to the hospital, which was not of Massachusetts General standards but which was a place of healing. At first the doctors were unwilling to let us see the matador, whose wound had been properly cleaned and sutured, but when Don Eduardo, at Judy's insistence, said that he was sure Victoriano would want to see her, they surrendered: "Well, he is in stable condition. Just a normal bullfighter's bad luck. His leg will be back to normal sooner than you'd think," and our delegation was led to his room, private and the best the hospital could provide.

The matador was awake. He was in surprisingly good condition. The doctors were right, the horn had stabbed deep but had missed vital parts, especially the intestines, so that it could be treated as a normal flesh wound. Penicillin would keep any poisons from the horn tip localized and neutralized. Pale from the shock of being hit so hard, Victoriano was now relaxed and even able to speculate on how soon he might return to the ring: "Not next week, for sure, and then our season's over in Mexico. But a restful sea trip to Spain, I'll be ready for their season." He had already given Veneno instructions to protect the Madrid and Barcelona contracts.

Much as I knew about bullfighters, I was startled by the young man's determination to resume control of his career. His life was to fight bulls and his obligation to himself and his profession was to mend and get back into the ring as soon as possible. This he would do, and as I looked at him lying there in the healing position the average man would want to maintain for a week or two, until all tissues were safely mended, I realized how different bullfighters were from ordinary men: if their guts had not been torn apart by the horn, they wanted to be up and about.

Don Eduardo, having arranged for us to get into the room, felt his duty discharged and excused himself: "Work to do. I'll send the car back to wait for you," and he went to the bed, smoothed the matador's hair, and patted him on the cheek: "You'll be walking in three days, Maestro," and with that benediction he was gone.

So now it was Victoriano in bed, Judy sitting on the edge of the bed, and me watching from the room's lone chair. As soon as Don Eduardo disappeared, Judy kissed her matador ardently, throwing her arms about his shoulders, while I looked at the ceiling. "You'll be fine for Spain," she said. "Do you want me to come with you?"

"*No es posible*," he said with surprising vigor. "In Spain I have much work to do."

"But you'll also need someone to look after you," and he said: "Veneno does that. You'd find no time to be with me."

"I'd find time. I found time tonight, didn't I?"

He was so deeply touched by her eagerness to share his misfortune that he edged himself to a sitting position, freed his arms, and embraced her heartily, while I winced as if I had the pain, not he. It was a long embrace and in no way a formal greeting or acknowledgment. This pair meant it, and I cannot now recall who made the next suggestion, maybe it was both of them, but someone said: "Could you wait in the hall?" and out I went.

The hospital had a waiting room, a forlorn place with a few tattered magazines, but as I tried to interest myself in them my eyes refused to focus, for I was imagining the scene back in the room. The indignity that I was being subjected to by a young woman whom I had known far better than the matador ever would, was so humiliating that I started to rebel, thinking that I should walk back to the Terrace and leave the car for her, but before I could make this flamboyant gesture I fell asleep.

I cannot say how long Judy was alone with her matador, perhaps an hour, for I had been very tired with nights of revelry and days of exciting revisits to old scenes, but when she shook me and said: "That's it. Let's get going," it took me a few moments to figure out where I was. But on the ride back to the hotel I came totally awake, for Judy kept grasping my arm and saying: "Oh, Clay! He's such a man! Worth the whole trip to Mexico." And when we were back at a table on the Terrace she was so eager to talk that I remained with her as she told me: "When the idea of this trip first came up back at school, I had a premonition that it was something I ought to do... was even driven to do. That it could prove very important. During the first days I found nothing special, just a lively weekend. But with him it all changed."

"You've known him two days."

"It's the nights that count."

"So you're going to chase after him, all over Spain?"

"No, I'm going back to Dallas and marry Harrison Caddy."

I was astounded: "H.C. on the shaving gear?"

"I was sorry you had to see that. Yes, Harrison Caddy. Sounds like a Martin and Lewis comedy doesn't it?" When in my meanness I said that it did, she snapped: "He'll buy your publisher and fire you."

"Victoriano gave a gallant fight, didn't he?"

"Yes, and I rewarded him. And now that I know what men are all about I'm ready to marry one who may not be a world beater but who strikes a pretty fair average." She drew back, studied me and said: "You didn't strike such a bad average yourself. Not totally disappointing."

"Considering that I lacked the dough to buy the company."

"Don't sneer at such a deficiency. It does count."

When we reached the Terrace she hurried directly to her room: "We leave at eight. Long drive north, and since I'll be driving, I need my sleep."

"Sleep well," and she pressed my arm: "I will. Ten more minutes of this Toledo stuff, I'll fall asleep here, standing up, the way you did."

As I led her to the stairs I became aware that someone behind a big vase of flowers was whispering my name and when I went to see, it was Betsy King. "What's the secret?" I asked, and she put her fingers to her lips: "Is he still out there?"

"Who?"

"That guy with the sticks?"

When I moved slowly back to where I could survey the Terrace I saw that Flaco Flores, the skinny *banderillero* who had placed that sensational pair, was seated alone at the far table reserved for Juan Gómez and his troupe. Returning to Betsy I said: "Yes, his name is Flaco Flores, if that's any help. Is he waiting for you?"

"He thinks he is."

"And you?"

"I'm waiting for that neat matador we met out at the ranch. The one who helped me."

"Gustavo Morones?"

"Is that his name?"

"It is, but that's of no interest to you, because you have a date with Flaco," and I started to drag her out onto the Terrace, but to my surprise she executed a defensive maneuver she had learned when, with other college girls, she frequented the honky-tonks of Fort Worth. Giving me a practiced knee where it hurt most, she snarled in a rot-gut voice I could scarcely believe, since she had seemed so school-girl sweet when I met her: "You try that again, Bubba, you'll sing soprano the rest of your life."

"You're standing that man up? After he dedicated that tremendous pair to you?" When she refused to answer, I asked in a sharp whisper: "Do you realize what he did for you. A complete turn within the cradle of the horns? Damn it, you owe him his date, because you'll never get a gift like that for the rest of your life."

"Did you see that beat-up cape he gave me to watch? The guy's a born loser."

I wanted to slap her for this dismissal of a decent man with whom she'd spent the night before, but there was that honky-tonk knee again and the biting suggestion: "Why don't you go play with your own age group, Grand Pops?" so I left her, but when I returned to the Terrace I was faced with an equally difficult situation. At the far table which had pre-

Pepe Luis Vásquez

viously been occupied by Matador Juan Gómez, who
was now in the hospital getting his leg attended to
with penicillin and stitches, I saw his hired *banderillero* Flaco Flores sitting alone.* He looked so forlorn
that I joined him: "¿Que tal, amigo?" and he related
a mournful tale: "Señorita Betsy said she would meet
me here again tonight. Domingo. She speaks good
Spanish. She knows."

"That was a magnificent pair, Flaco."

He brightened: "Did you catch? The turn, I
mean?"

"I was using instant film advance. Maybe six

---

*Unwittingly, I had used almost the same words on a previous page,
but such repetition can be detected and changed during editing.

shots in a row."

"That could be good."

"If they're as good as I hope, we might run all six across the two pages. '¡Así Banderillean los Grandes! (How the Great Ones Place the Sticks).

"You'll send me copies? Maybe six?"

"I promise, because that pair was fine."

"What do you think happened to the señorita?"

"If she said she'd be here, she will," I lied.

And here she came on the arm of Gustavo Montaño*, the full matador who had assisted her at Don Eduardo's fiesta that afternoon. Casting only a furtive eye at Flaco, she allowed Montaño to seat her at the big table in the center to which another *torero* and his girl came to make a handsome and noisy quartet.

Flaco paled when he saw what she had done and started to rise as if to challenge the matador, but I put out a restraining hand and a brawl was averted. But even so, I suppose it would not have happened, for when Flaco reconsidered I could see that he realized that one of these days he might want to seek employment from Montaño. Furthermore, a *banderillero* does not challenge any matador, not if he has good sense.

Distraught, the skinny man who would have spent most of his afternoon's earnings to entertain Miss Betsy from Dallas sat glumly beside me staring at her table. Then abruptly, and with a great show of movement, he half-rose and turned his chair so

---

*I had trouble with this young man's name and tried several variations before I settled on Morones. Montaño is a carry-over from an earlier print-out as are the variances between González and Gonzales.

that he faced not Betsy and her matador but the corner cafe in which his matador's girl, Lucha González was singing. Aware from the corner of his eye that Betsy had ignored his attempt at rebuffing her, didn't even see it, he could take no more. Leaping from his chair and starting for the other table, he would have destroyed himself in bullfight circles had I not anticipated his move, risen with him, and with a commanding grip on his left arm steered him quietly away from where the two matadors sat with their girls. No one at the table, least of all Betsy, was aware of how close to disaster they had been, nor did anyone there look up to watch what I was doing.

When I had him well clear of the Terrace I stopped him under a lamplight, relaxed my grip and asked: "Were you going to hit him?"

"He stole her."

I felt qualified to say that sometimes a man has to watch in silence as someone waltzes off with his woman, and reluctantly he agreed: "Maybe I shouldn't have been there. A place like that is for matadors."

"With a pair like yours today, you can sit anywhere. But now what?"

"Who knows? With Gómez wounded, I don't know. I don't get many fights."

"How many a season?"

"Maybe five. I think that pair today, if any of the newspapers print it, that might help."

"Flaco, if my shots turn out, and I print that series of six photos of you, you'll get a lot more than five."

"Don't lose the film."

"And now what?"

"I have to get my gear. My cape, a fine old one,

borrowed from a man in Guadalajara. A bull caught him, he don't fight anymore."

"And when you get your stuff?"

"I go to the station where the trucks leave for Guadalajara. The drivers know me. The Sunday night runs. I'll be home by dawn."

"Flaco, I'm going to earn a lot of money on those shots of you. Let me give you your share now."

Proudly he refused: "I get by. My mother lets me live with her. I do all right."

"Flaco, damn it. You earned the money. It's your legal share."

"You mean, like a salary?" For this question he used an old Spanish word, *sueldo,* and I said eagerly: "That's it, your *sueldo,*" and with a dignity which made me ashamed to look in his eyes, he accepted two ten dollar bills.

The resolution of Professor Longford's case was difficult, the relevant passages being:

Yet I did want to talk and so did she, so I asked her to share a brief summary of the observations she'd been making about American courtship patterns: "This festival has been a revelation, Norman. When you're in a university setting in Dallas and two of your most challenging students tell you: 'We're going to hightail it down to Mexico and see if we can land us a couple of matadors,' I thought, with my upbringing, that this was no more than a colorful idiom. I didn't dream the words meant just what they said. Those kids would have used lariats to catch themselves bullfighters, and I've been wondering, as these hectic days passed: 'Do the rest of my women students think in similar terms?'"

She laughed at her disclosures, then added one

that startled me in its frankness. I'd have expected it from Judy, but not from her: "I suppose that when the three of us get back on campus we could say of this excursion: 'We went to Mexico to catch us some matadors, and we damned well did. All three of us.'"

"Ricardo Martín?"

"Yes."

"When you went upstairs with him the other night. . . ."

"Talk. Profound talk from a young man in whom I could become intensely interested." She shifted in her chair and changed the quality of her voice: "I've never in my life conceded that I could one day be so man-hungry that I'd be interested in some boy younger than myself. Me twenty-six, him twenty-four. I felt like Sam Goldwyn when someone asked him what the chances were on a movie deal: 'I can tell you in two words, Oom-possible.'"

"You didn't answer my question about the other night."

"I didn't because you had no right to ask it."

I was so taken by the way she was discussing her role in the festival, that I placed my hands over hers and said: "You may have something important to say in your study, if you can get it down on paper. You're very bright, indeed. Another time, another place . . . ."

She shook her head, almost in anger, "It's strange. I come to this unlikely place and three totally desirable men, none of them married, tell me that under the right circumstances. . . . Why doesn't anyone tell me that in Dallas when the circumstances are right?"

"Ricardo, me and who's the third?"

"This big one," she said, pointing to the caped

figure of León Ledesma as he made his way to our table. When he reached us I said: "This young woman has been telling me you made a pass at her. Join the club."

"What I said was that if she moved to Toledo, and found a good paying job, and converted to Catholicism, and learned idiomatic Spanish, I might, I just might, develop an interest in her. What I meant was that I'd give her a fighting chance to prove herself . . . ."

We had settled nothing when we heard an insistent horn, and there was Judy Hooper in her convertible, blowing like mad. When she attracted our attention she called: "Liz, we leave in twelve minutes. I've paid the hotel bills. Grab your stuff and get down here, because at oh-eight-hundred I head north." When Liz dashed into the hotel, Judy shouted: "You, Clay! Go up and get that red-head down here, now! Because I'm leaving."

As I ran into the hotel I saw Judy giving Ledesma a kiss and sharing the latest gossip with him, but I forgot such things when I reached Betsy King's room, for when I pushed open the door to roust her out of bed and help her pack, I found that she was not alone. A very handsome young matador lay there with her, a vivid scar showing across his naked chest.

Attempting no apologies, I cried: "Your car leaves in ten minutes! Here!" and I threw her a towel. I've often recalled the next frantic minutes with a half-dressed Betsy dashing about and tossing me things to pack, while Gustavo Morones remained placidly in bed, watching us with a half-smile. I think if he'd said one word I'd have tried to slug him, despite our difference in ages, and I like to think that because I was in better physical shape than he, I might have got away with it.

Pushing Betsy toward the door, then waiting as

she ran back to kiss him goodbye, I listened as she said the damnedest thing: "Come June, I'll be in Madrid, Junior Year Abroad, it'll be in the phone book. If you get the contracts you said, I'd like to see Spain with you." And in those few seconds a transatlantic love affair was arranged. He did not get out of bed to kiss her goodbye.

After I had tucked her gear into the convertible I assumed that my duties with the Texas girls were over, but not quite. Judy left the car, grabbed my hands and gave me a no-fooling kiss. Then the professor did the same, and even Betsy leaned out and kissed me, once again the shy, sweet kid she'd been three days ago, but I could not let her get away with it. Grabbing her by the arm I said: "When my article comes out with those six great shots of Flaco placing his *banderillas* for you, cut the strip out and paste it on your wardrobe to remind you he risked his life to honor you. You'll be lucky if your matador ever does anything half as important," and in her nineteen-year-old little-girl voice she promised: "I'll do just that, Grand Pops."

Judy of course had the last word: "You've been a champion, Clay. We couldn't have done it without you and your matadors." As the convertible started to move I cried: "Kids! Be careful. We don't want to lose you," and rarely have I spoken more from the heart.

The final comments on the Texas girls came from the uncle of the narrator, Don Eduardo Palafox, the distinguished breeder of fighting bulls and the man who had arranged the *tienta* on his ranch. When he encountered his nephew on Monday morning he snarled: "Your behavior's been abominable, a disgrace to the Palafox name. So if you bother to return for our Festival next year, don't you dare bring your Texas *putas*. Doing it in a public hospital . . . the nurses called me."

But later, in a more amiable mood, he wrote to Clay in a conciliatory tone:

> Our entire committee feels it would add a great deal to Ixmiq-62 if you could attend as a highly regarded son of Toledo, and it would be even better if you would persuade those three wonderful girls from Texas to return. They made a most favorable impression on the men of our committee, especially the two girls who fought our cows with such style.
>
> Your Admiring Uncle Eduardo

VII. BENNETT CERF REDIVIVUS

From the passages cited it is obvious, I hope, that I wrote Chapters 11 through 17 with affection for the three Texas girls, but also with a desire to explain a phenomenon which I'd observed around the world: a coterie which was becoming known in the vernacular as 'groupies,' gangs of uninhibited girls and young women who cluster about athletic heroes and other celebrities, often hoping to bed with them. In the Mexican bullfight scene when I knew it well, they were conspicuous and rather difficult to fathom.

I strove to present my young women honestly, without exaggeration or ridicule. I certainly did not depict them as occupying the bottom layer of this obstreperous breed but rather the likable young women who seek adventure before settling down to ordinary marriages. I thought of them as acceptable heroines and still do.

But I was about to receive a shock. When my editors in New York, having been enthusiastic about my original ten chapters, read the later seven, they were unanimous in rejecting the three Texans. They advised me to drop them from the manuscript, not to waste time trying to modify them, and to proceed with the job of redrafting the final chapters without their presence: 'They do not fit. They're an intrusion that adds nothing to the inherent movement of the novel.' Their rejection was so firm that it did not allow counter-debate, and while I was not bound to accept their negative judgment, it had been delivered with such clarity that I would have been foolish to ignore it. But in accepting it, I faced problems of considerable philosophical and structural complexity.

When I endeavored to digest this negative criticism I concluded that it was my presenting them as groupies that had offended. I suspected that women editors had found the Texas girls distasteful and even grossly immoral, but I was not then in a position from which I could rebut them by pointing out that the behavior of my characters was normal within their category, and even reserved. But then, in 1991-92, a bizarre series of incidents brought the problem of groupies into the headlines, proving that what I had written about my Texas girls was actually quite temperate.

First, Magic Johnson, the charismatic wonder-star of professional basketball and a most likable young man, confessed publicly that he had acquired the HIV virus that almost always leads to fatal AIDS. He admitted that he had probably contracted the virus through the careless sex habits commonly indulged in by professional athletes and gave a shocking interview in which he said that he had tried to accommodate as many women as possible.

Second, Wilt Chamberlain, the giant basketball player who performed miracles on the court and once scored a hundred points in one game, boasted that he had enjoyed sex with about 20,000 different women.

Third, when Mike Tyson, a ferocious boxer who annihilated his opponents, was found guilty of raping a young beauty-queen contestant, comments during his trial focused on the fact that as a champion prize fighter he was accustomed to the adulation of women and that his behavior with Miss Washington was not extraordinary—he said that she should have expected it when she dated him late at night and under ominous circumstances.

Fourth, Martina Navratilova, the tennis champion who has had a well-publicized sex life involving a court case brought against her, gave a daring but splendid public statement in which she complained that the public was making a moral hero of Magic Johnson for the moving and commendable way he had confessed on television regarding his affliction, while if she, or any other woman athlete, had revealed promiscuous behavior, she would have been branded a prostitute and been ostracized.

Fifth, these four highly publicized incidents encouraged several sports writers to reflect publicly on the fact that an ambience has grown up within the world of professional sports which condones treating groupies as available game. Other writers ventilated the scandals that often occur in college and university sports in which gang rapes seem to be acceptable behavior for athletes; others reported cases in which well regarded male college athletes raped female students and were protected by college authorities who either did not prosecute the charges of rape, or who applied pressure on the young women to persuade them to retract their charges.

From the time I wrote my account of the Texas groupies— and they did not really warrant that pejorative term—to the weeks in 1992 when I tried to decide whether to erase them, the climate of public opinion had changed so radically that at first I believed I ought to barge ahead with the seven chapters as written. They were honest, they represented the scene without violence or offensive sex, and they added to the portrait of a Mexican festival. I decided to keep them, if Random House would allow me to do so.

But then I began to wonder if my first reactions to the negative comment were justified. Did the criticism of the three Texas girls really focus on their sexual behavior, or was it possible that my critics did not like the girls because their intrusion negatively affected the forward movement of the narrative? More important, did they preempt so much space and attention that I was not handling adequately the problems of my main characters: my narrator and his problem of what to do with the remainder of his life; and my premier matador who sought to return to the days when he was his own man and not a plastic creation of his domineering father and his two brothers?

Then, one afternoon as I wandered by a Florida waterway filled with egrets, herons and rowdy pelicans, a startling thought struck me: 'These Random House editors today are saying exactly what Bennett Cerf, another Random House official, said thirty years ago: "The intrusion of those Hollywood types does nothing to help your novel. Instead they impede it. Get rid of them."' Now, though long dead, he was warning me from the grave and through the agency of editors he had never met or even known about: 'Cut the Texas girls. They're a diversion. They do nothing to enhance the novel. Instead they detract from your main story, the effect of the festival on your major characters.'

When I phrased it that way or, more accurately, when I saw it more clearly, I could see that Cerf had been right in 1961, which was why I dropped the novel then, and his advice still applied. But there was a vast difference between the two occasions. Then I had been a beginning writer feeling my way down a dangerous path—the writing of long novels involving many centuries and many generations of characters—and I was neither strong enough to accept negative criticism from my publisher, nor experienced enough to see how, if I did accept it, I could revise the entire plan for the novel. I had allowed him to derail me.

But now I was a tough old bird, veteran of many writing and publishing experiences, so that when my editors said firmly: 'This is wrong' I knew how to accept that criticism, regroup my energies and redo the final chapters till they were right.

Once I accepted the criticism and admitted its propriety— that my beloved Texas girls were an intrusion and a deviation— I had no hesitation in bidding them farewell. Lovely Judy Hooker, brilliant Professor Longford, rowdy red-headed Betsy King, farewell. In another time, in another place . . . as one of the characters in the novel had said.

I spent long hours over many days wandering along the waterway—in Maine I walk under majestic pine trees for nature has always been my therapy—trying to sort out the values involved in what I had to do. The first decision came easily. If the Texans had to go, I already had in the novel a group of seven

Oklahomans ready to replace them. They could be cut back to five, among whom would be Penny, a delightful seventeen-year-old daughter of a Tulsa oil millionaire, ready-made to substitute for Judy Hooker, but on a lower octane level. I awaited her eagerly and preened when she turned out to be a delectable addition, western-pretty but also strong-willed.

It became clear that I could transfer to Penny, making proper adjustments since her personality was much different from Judy's, many of the interesting exploits in which Judy had been involved, but making her a restrained, well-behaved young woman instead of an avid bed-hopper. She cooperated—readers of *Mexico* will recognize several short passages from *The Texas Girls* which have been altered to fit her—and the novel was strengthened.

In the space thus made available by dropping the other two Texans, I could pay closer attention to my main protagonists, the American newsman and the matadors, and this treatment enabled me to make them men of much stronger character and significance. And by cutting down the number of Oklahomans, I had space to develop more fully those I kept.

Thus the ghostly voice of my old friend, Bennett Cerf, speaking in echoing whispers, encouraged me to go back to where he left me in 1961, make the changes he had recommended then, and produce a better book both for myself and for the company he had brought into being.

I still had much work to do in actually writing the new chapters and then coordinating them with the earlier ones. So much had changed in thirty years. For example, as a beginner I had used traditional methods for handling dialogue:

> In response he said, "I'll be leaving at ten."

But the more I wrote, the more tedious I found it to be repeating endlessly *he said* and had adopted a much better solution:

> He could not agree: 'I'll be leaving at ten.'

and often I give the quote without bothering to indicate who is speaking, a practice which annoys my copy editors and which, under pressure in specific examples where clarity has been obscured, I abandon. Also I now prefer one quotation mark (') rather than two (").

More important were the changes in my characters' motivations, the weight given to certain ideas, altered details in Mexican life and customs, and the mysterious values accorded to certain arts or concepts. All those required changes in the first ten chapters, for I was not now the man I was when I wrote the beginnings of my novel, nor did I see things the same way, but the distant beginnings which were right also modified what I now wrote. It was a process of endless change, fore and aft.

I have always experimented in names, frequently changing them in the middle of a chapter if they lacked the proper resonance. In doing this I had finally found several which gained acceptance among my readers: Nellie Forbush seems exactly right for a navy nurse from Arkansas. Pasquinel was a fine invention for a French fur trapper; indeed, it was such an echoing name that a saloon keeper in Scotland asked my permission to name his bistro after the Frenchman, while a posh restaurant in Greeley, Colorado, is named after Potato Brumbaugh. In *Mexico* I altered names rapidly until I found ones with which I could live, and that required constant changing in the two texts.

And there were minor oddities. In the original I denoted word accents in this widely accepted way: 'Richard Martin, the American lad from San Diego who aspired to be a bullfighter, changed his name to Ricardo Martín (Mar-TEEN).' When I saw those big letters glaring at me from one of my books they offended me. I now use Martín (Mar-teén) and like it better. Also, now when I must quote a substantial passage from another source, I prefer to put it in a blocked body of text, single spaced, double indented both left and right, but with no added indentation to indicate the beginning of the quoted passage. And when resuming normal double-spaced text, I like it to be flush left, again with no indication of the paragraph. In a series of either words or phrases separated by commas I now prefer to drop the final comma unless meaning demands it. Proofreading *Mexico* was not easy, and for the sake of stylistic harmony the new chapters were recast in my old styles.

There was also the problem presented by the three very long chapters dealing with my narrator's Indian, Spanish and American ancestors. It soon became obvious that good book-making required that each be cut into parts at historical points where they should have been cut anyway. Also, the poetic Chapter 13 *By Torchlight* in the structure I had developed in 1991, had already been interchanged with Chapter 14 *American Ancestors*, so that as I started my revision the chapter sequence agreed upon was:

8. JAM 1992

1. Cactus and Maguey
2. The Spaniard
3. The Rancher
4. The Indian
5. Indian Ancestors: The Builders
6. Indian Ancestors: The Altomecs
7. The Critic
8. Friday Fight
9. Meaning of Death
10. Spanish Ancestors: In Spain
11. Spanish Ancestors: In Mexico
12. The Barbers
13. On the Terrace
14. Fight #2: Saturnine Saturday
15. American Ancestors: In Virginia
16. American Ancestors: In Mexico
17. By Torchlight
18. The Sorteo
19. Fight #3: Sol y Sombra
20. House of Tile

How many changes there had been between the first outline and the last! And how many of them came late in this intricate process!

Even with the outline firmly in mind, the actual writing of the chapters did not come easily. The records at the end of each chapter, as typed out by my word-processing secretaries—six of them at different times and in different cities because I was moving around so much—show that on certain difficult chapters as many as seven revisions were needed to nail down what was required, and all the chapters went through three or four major revisions after which came editorial work in New York, proofreading at Random House and further proofreading by me. Finally it was ready for the printer.

I had every reason to believe that the perilous and oft-diverted journey of this manuscript had been safely accomplished, for it was now out of my hands, but even as I contemplated its completion with satisfaction, a phone call reached me from Guadalajara. It was from a dear and highly regarded woman with whom I'd had an admiring friendship dating back many decades in both Mexico and Portugal. She was Conchita Cintrón, the world's most famous woman bullfighter, a *rejoneadora* who fought bulls from horseback, using a long-handled *rejón* (lance).

The mistress of this arcane skill wanted to ask me a question about a visit we'd had when she was performing in Portugal. As I heard her enthusiastic voice again, speaking in good English—for her father had been a Puerto Rican cavalry officer who attended West Point and married an American girl— she seemed to come riding right into my room astride her white horse who knelt before me so that his mistress could cry: 'Don Jaime! There must be a place for us in your novel!' and as she smiled an idea leaped into my mind: 'She'd be ideal as the opener for my second fight in Ixmiq-61. A marvelous woman to counterbalance the plethora of men fighters. We'd also be able to observe Penny's reactions to this woman champion.'

When her telephone call ended, I hurried to my typewriter, bade a regretful farewell to my other bullfight friend, Gastón Santos, and redrafted the scenes in which he had appeared with his customary charm and bravura. I was sorry to lose him, particularly after rediscovering his name lost thirty years ago, but was overjoyed to include the great Conchita, for she was indeed *Númera Una*, if I am allowed to feminize that popular phrase. She had galloped into the heart of my novel.

Conchita Cintrón, Rejoneadora Número Una

In these strange and arbitrary ways this manuscript, which had refused to die, persevered to a satisfactory life. As a published book it would find new adventures: a wide readership, selection as a major book club choice, publication in more than a dozen languages throughout the world, and a secure place in the hearts of people who had an affinity for Mexico. The efforts of the gifted women who have assisted me so ably: my cousin Virginia in finding the manuscript; Kate and Olga and Sono and Carole of Random House who labored over the pages; my six secretaries who, at one time or another and in various places did the typing and the word processing—Evelyn in Doylestown, Nadia in Kintnersville, Theresa in Miami, Debbie and Dena and Maggie in Austin—came wonderfully to fulfillment.

But there was also a sardonic aspect to this sometimes frenzied work, and an explanation should give courage to the beginning writer. Toward the end of my writing career, managerial affairs at Random House, my long-time publisher with whom I'd had the most congenial relations, began to fall into temporary disarray. Specialists with whom I had worked were fired or retired. Branches of the house which had brought the company prestige were juggled about, and men with fine reputations in the industry were let go, sometimes in unacceptable ways. Outraged writers paraded in the street, threats were made, and at the height of the affair I published a letter in which I said that if this continued I would move two manuscripts I had already finished to another publisher.

When Studs Terkel, the brilliant brawler from Chicago who was leading the public protest against Random, thought that I had already made the switch, he telephoned to congratulate me on the move, and other dissidents did the same. Eager to carry out the threat I had made, but saddened by the impasse into which my publisher had fallen, I asked my agent, Owen

Laster, to take my two manuscripts to other publishers: 'And you can tell them that I feel so strongly about this that I will be willing to accept a modest royalty.' Having made the generous, honorable gesture, I sat back, waiting to see which major house would grab at the two completed manuscripts, one *The Novel* about the Pennsylvania Dutch around Lancaster, and the other a kind of summary autobiography, *The World Is My Home.*

To my astonishment, considering my track record of decades of successful publishing, no house wanted the manuscripts. The first firm which Laster approached, a magisterial place, said: 'We would not care to publish either book.' The second, almost as famous, conceded: 'We might consider the autobiography but would not care for the other, since it has no merit and deals with events long past.' Humiliated, I myself took the project to a third house, one with younger editors and bright hopes. They said, not directly but in terms that could not be misinterpreted: 'Michener is a nice fellow, but his day is passed. We're into whole new areas,' and with that brush-off they let me know they did not even care to inspect the manuscripts.

These present paragraphs are, therefore, a kind of apology to Terkel: 'Studs, I took your phone call seriously. I wanted to support your gesture in defense of responsible publishing. I took my two manuscripts to other publishers and found I could not give the damned things away. I tried to support you, but was denied the opportunity.'

As I reflected upon this mortifying experience I concluded that the three publishers, who not only rejected but in a sense despised my manuscripts, were correct in their decisions to decline them. The potential books were not of sufficient worth to justify a wrestling match with Random House. The manuscripts were outside the pattern which had accounted for that impressive string of big bestsellers which had characterized my earlier writing. And the young editors were right: I was a has-been. I had been willing almost to give the books away and had found no takers.

At this painful juncture I had no recourse but to return to Random House and ask: 'Do you still want to publish them?' When I posed this question I was in Washington attending an important meeting of a committee on which I served regarding foreign affairs, but the two heads of Random House, the owner Si Newhouse and his publisher Alberto Vitale, flew down for a tense three-hour meeting in which we discussed fundamentals. I assured them that I still wanted to publish with Random if they were interested in carrying on the traditions of that great house and they assured me that that was their intention. We discussed the fact that the publishing costs of my early books had been recouped once the books sold around eight thousand copies: 'So it's clear that if one ultimately sells eight hundred thousand, the publisher is making a fortune. If that windfall is not ploughed back in the form of support for beginning writers, the efforts of the older, successful writer have been in vain.' They assured me that they understood this better than I and that profits were being placed back into the mainstream of publishing. With those understandings we shook hands. I returned to my meetings and they flew back to New York.

The next day one of the newspapers carried the sardonic headline: 'MICHENER TALKING, NOT WALKING,' and the affair ended to the disgust of those other writers who had hoped that I would leave Random House.

Now the denouement. *The Novel* was published. I'm told it was blasted by several major critics, which justified the three publishers who rejected it as worthless. But it was also received with acclaim by others and resided a respectable time on the bestseller lists. Several publishers wrote to inform me that they had asked their staffs to read the book as an honest portrait of the writing and publishing experience. Correspondents like it.

The World Is My Home was published to wide, if guarded acclaim, found a home on the bestseller lists, never at the top but in the respectable suburbs, and evoked a flood of letters from readers who judged it one of my best efforts. I expect it to enjoy a long and increasingly valued life.

But the amusing aspect of all this is that had any one of those three publishers accepted instead of rejected the two manuscripts when I tried to give them away, they would in time have automatically inherited not only my novel *Mexico* but also another novel I've been working on for some time. Focused on a wholly new theme of critical relevance, it could turn out to be the best I will ever write. If *Mexico* and the new manuscript achieve wide readership, the three publishers will have thrown away a minor gold mine.

The history of publishing is replete with instances in which a knowledgeable editor baby-sits some struggling writer through several disappointing early books, only to cut him or her loose just as the next book is ready to prove a tremendous success. The dramatic cases of John Irving and Leon Uris come to mind. The beginner can take comfort from my experience: 'When he was eighty-five Jim Michener could not give away his manuscripts. They said he was too old, too out of date. But they became bestsellers in languages all over the globe.' Sometimes it is the writer, not the publisher, who knows what makes a viable book.